A CATALOG OF THE CURIOUS

May 1961. Giant bird, prehistoric looking, approaches an aircraft over the Hudson River in New York.

August 1963. Forty-foot sea monster reported off the coast of New Jersey.

June 1961. Blood spots keep reappearing at a house in Houston, Texas.

August 1973. Over 50 encounters reported of "smelly" nine-foot tall humanoids.

July 1972. Statue of the Virgin Mary weeps in New Orleans, Louisiana.

October 1973. Two local residents of Pescagoula, Mississippi, are taken aboard a strange craft where they talk with aliens. Both men later pass lie detector tests.

July 1962. Numerous windows are broken in San Bernardino, California, when pebbles rain down.

**These are only a few
of the unexplainable events in . . .**

BIZARRE AMERICA

BEYOND BELIEF:

BIZARRE AMERICA

GERRY HUNT

Senior Researcher
MARTINA VERA

BERKLEY BOOKS, NEW YORK

To

Robin Leach, Stephen Rosenberg and Norfolk Punch

and

Mickey

BEYOND BELIEF: BIZARRE AMERICA

A Berkley Book / published by arrangement with
the author

PRINTING HISTORY
Berkley edition/December 1988

ISBN: 0-425-10849-X

A BERKLEY BOOK ® TM 757,375
Berkley Books are published by The Berkley Publishing Group,
200 Madison Avenue, New York, N.Y. 10016.
The name "BERKLEY" and the "B" logo
are trademarks belonging to Berkley Publishing Corporation.

PRINTED IN THE UNITED STATES OF AMERICA

10 9 8 7 6 5 4 3 2 1

Acknowledgments

My sincere thanks especially to William R. Corliss, one of the country's most noted specialists in the gathering of unusual natural phenomena, for his help and guidance. Appreciation is also expressed to an exceptional scientist, Professor Michael A. Persinger, Ph.D., of Laurentian University.

Martina Vera's researching skills were greatly appreciated.

Table of Contents

INTRODUCTION

Of Strange Little Men

He appeared out of nowhere—a little peach-colored person, no bigger than the average family dog, crouched atop a low stone wall.

The little man slinked on all fours across the loose, large stones that made up the wall, though "all fours" might not give quite the right impression, since he possessed hands with extraordinarily long fingers. His arms were skinny, his legs spindly. He had a bulbous head and saucer-shaped, lidless eyes which, when the high beams from a passing car caught him in their glare, glowed a bright fluorescent orange. Strangely enough, there was no apparent signs of a nose, mouth, or ears.

The creature wasn't wearing a stitch of clothing, and the peachy hue of his hairless and shiny skin gave him the appearance of a shaved, but grotesquely misproportioned chimpanzee. Nobody who saw him can quite remember exactly how he reacted in the full glare of the headlights, except that he seemed to tighten the grip of one hand around a large stone on top of the wall, possibly in surprise or to steady himself. Despite the tension in his stance, however, he seemed in no hurry, and merely turned his head slowly away from the oncoming car.

Whoever or whatever this creature was, it is estimated that, if erect, he would have been between three and four feet tall. One thing was certain; his head, on a short, skinny neck, appeared to outweigh the rest of his body, much the way a human fetus looks as it begins its major stages of development in the womb.

The three teenagers in the car, Mike Mazzocca, Bill Bartlett, and Andrew Brodie, all seventeen-year-olds, were the first to spot him—the Dover Demon. Their reaction was disbelief, shock, and then . . . abject fear.

A lonely country road, a bizarre pink humanoid, and a group of teenagers out for a joyride who are scared so witless, they will begin to question their own sanity. Where was all this happening? It was taking place in Dover, Massachusetts, a small suburb of Boston. Shrouded in woodlands, Dover is a natural oasis of nature, some fifteen miles southwest of the harum-scarum world of the "Teaport." It's no hillbilly country with superstitions and tall tales, either; it's one of the swankiest places to live in Massachusetts, with a per capita income higher than most every other town in the state.

The little creature was later to become known as the Dover Demon. And with good reason. This was not its only appearance during a twenty-four-hour period on April 21-22, 1977. Some two hours later, shortly after the teenagers' hair-raising, midnight experience, another close encounter was to take place.

The Demon had first been spotted on Farm Street. Just one mile away, across some heavily wooded land is Millers Hill Road, another quiet and mostly deserted rural highway. A fifteen-year-old youth, John Baxter, who had left his girl friend's house about half an hour before, was walking on Millers Hill Road when something up ahead caught his eye. What he thought he saw was the silhouette of a small child approaching along the narrow country lane.

There was no moonlight, since the sky was overcast, and visibility in the early morning darkness was poor. It struck Baxter as odd that a child would be out at this time of night. As the figure drew nearer, however, Baxter was increasingly unsure as to what exactly it was coming up in front of him. Its shape didn't look as much like a child as he'd first thought. In fact, it had a strange, loping gait, and looked like some sort of animal walking upright on two legs.

The figure stopped, and Baxter stopped. Baxter called out a greeting. There was no response, so Baxter tried again and took one more step forward. The figure, now only about fifteen feet away from him, jumped sideways and went scurrying through a wooded thicket away from the road. Footsteps could be heard as the creature ran through the undergrowth, down a gully, across a marshy patch of land, and up a slight incline on the other side.

Baxter, in his bewilderment and curiosity, decided to give chase. When the creature came to a stop, Baxter spotted it about thirty feet away from him, across the gully, standing on a large rock next to a small tree. Even through the gloom Baxter was able to see that the creature had long fingers that were clutching the tree trunk for support. He noticed also its long, prehensile toes that clung firmly to the rock. Extending behind the creature was a large, open field and what moonlight there was created a silhouette. Whatever it was, it looked to Baxter to have a body similar to a monkey but with a much bigger, melon-shaped head. He saw the glint of two eyes, and felt as if the animal was observing him.

At this point the youth became apprehensive, afraid that the creature might be getting ready to pounce or attack. Baxter slowly backed up to the road, keeping the thing in view, and then took off running.

From the similarities in description and the coincidence of time and place, it would seem that this was the Dover Demon once again.

But wait. From the records, we find there was yet another sighting.

Twenty-four hours after the Baxter encounter, almost to the hour, young Will Taintor, eighteen, of Dover, was driving his girl friend Abby home. They were passing Trout Brook, just a little over a mile away from the sighting the night before on Millers Hill Road.

Abby, fifteen, was the first to notice something. Like the others, she caught a glimpse in the headlights of what she thought was an animal. Looking closer, she gasped. When questioned later, she was able to recall that the animal looked like a small, hairless ape crouched beside the road on all fours. She remembered the body as beige in color, but what stuck most in her mind was the impression that the head of the animal was disproportionately big for the body. And she swore that it had two eyes which glowed in the headlights.

Abby cried out to Will and pointed frantically. At that point, by Will's account, the car was almost even with the strange creature, and he caught only a mere glance through the side window as the vehicle passed by. Will remembers his immediate impression that it definitely *wasn't* a dog. It had a large head, and appeared to be crouched at the side of the road with its front legs raised off the ground.

The young couple didn't stop to investigate or turn around. In fact, Abby implored Will to speed up and get away from the area as quickly as possible.

Did the Dover Demon exist? Or was he just a product of the fertile imaginations of a group of teenagers? As later investigations by police and researchers of the paranormal were to show, the Dover Demon was to raise more questions than they could answer—considerably more.

Tales of the appearance of strange creatures who resemble people or mutant animals go back to antiquity. The first accounts were recorded by the ancient Christian monks in Britain and on the continent. Because these monks were the clerics of their age and the limited few in society who had the ability to write and record for posterity, these accounts were rendered in great detail. Oftentimes quaint, and frequently too bizarre to make much sense, early tales of the unusual have been traditionally dismissed as fairy stories or the products of deranged minds. But tales of strange folk, demons, hobgoblins, and dwarfs are the backbone of our history of the supernatural. And so as general interest in the paranormal has risen—and as the scientific and academic communities have become more receptive to the examination of such phenomena—these early accounts have come to be seen in a new light.

Of course, demons and such just don't leap out from the hedgerows of high-tech modern America, as a matter of course. Certainly you wouldn't expect it to be happening on a quiet spring evening in 1977 in a respectable, upright town like Dover, Massachusetts. Or would you?

Tales of bizarre, unexplainable creatures actually abound throughout our land, and they go all the way back to the days of our earliest settlers. But few are quite so strange, or have carried such an aura of mystery, as a visitation to the little town of Aurora, Texas, at the end of the last century.

Strange News from Aurora

On April 17, 1897, newspaper wire services flashed an almost unbelievable story across country. A strange flying machine had crashed in the tiny village of Aurora, an obscure community forty-five miles northwest of Dallas. This was news, hot news, especially in a time when flying machines were unheard of.

But even more incredible was the report that the townsfolk had recovered from the crash site the body of a tiny man and were preparing to bury him after the wreckage had been examined and removed.

The *Dallas Morning News* of April 17 read:

Dateline: Aurora, Wise County, Texas. About six o'clock this morning the early risers of Aurora were astonished at the certain appearance of an airship which had been sailing through the county.

It was traveling due north and much nearer the earth than before. Evidently some of the machinery was out of order, so it was making speed of only ten or twelve mph and gradually settling down toward the earth. It sailed directly over the public square, and when it approached the north part of town it collided with the tower of Judge Proctor's windmill. It went into pieces with a terrific explosion, scattering debris over several acres of ground.

The explosion wrecked the windmill and a water tank and destroyed the judge's favorite flower garden. The pilot of the ship was supposed to have been the only one on board and while the remains are badly disfigured, enough of the original body has been picked up to show that he is not an inhabitant of this world. Papers found on his person were evidently a record of his travels and are written in some unknown hieroglyphics which cannot be deciphered. The ship was too badly wrecked to form any conclusions about its construction or motor power. It was built of an unknown metal, somewhat resembling a mixture of silver, and must have weighed several tons.

The town is full of people today who are viewing the wreck and gathering specimens of the strange metal from the debris. The pilot's funeral will take place at noon today.

The newspaper account was at first considered to be a hoax. But the next day, the *News* followed up on the incident with eyewitness accounts of the strange airship and its inhabitant.

A gentleman and a lady whose reputation for truthfulness cannot be assailed, swore that the bright light crossed the sky near Denton. The man said, "I first thought it was a meteor, but on closer examination discovered that it was moving slowly in a southeasterly direction. At this speed the ship continued its course for a few minutes and then almost with a jump, it started off at a terrific speed and disappeared in the southeast.

"I would describe the object as being cigar-shaped, about fifty-feet long, with a long beak or blade resembling a cutwater on a ship. At the point where the beak joined the main body, a powerful searchlight threw its rays far into the night ahead. A row of windows on the side threw out a smaller source of light which must have been stored electricity as there was no sign of smoke or a smokestack."

Lawyer J. Spence Bounds, of Hilsboro Hill, Texas, said he was driving home after visiting a client when "I was astonished by a brilliant flash of an electric searchlight, which passed directly over my buggy. I was almost frightened to death by it. My horse was also frightened and came near to overturning the buggy. He snorted, reared up, and plunged madly. My hair stood straight up. Fortunately, the light rested on us scarcely a second and glided along over the fields and suddenly turned upwards toward the heavens. Then I beheld about a thousand feet above me a huge, black monster from which a light emanated. It was in a shape something like a cigar. The searchlight was presently shut off,

*and a number of incandescent lights flashed around
the lower edge of the body."*

To add to the impact of the whole affair, the Aurora
incident happened at the end of a ten-day period in which
hundreds of sightings of strange objects in the sky had been
reported from across the length and breadth of the country.

After suffering the indignity of being put up to ridicule
by the rest of the world, the residents of Aurora became
outraged when to add insult to injury, their quiet town was
invaded by hordes of curious sightseers grabbing anything
and everything they could that looked as if it might have
come from the bizarre craft. The town was turned upside
down in a morbid treasure hunt, as strangers went on the
rampage to search for the grave of the little creature who
had flown the ship. Every single plot of earth that looked
as if it could have been freshly dug (and some that obviously weren't) was ripped up. What the invaders didn't
know was that the town elders had buried what was left of
their little visitor in an obscure corner of the Aurora cemetery—the last place they figured anybody would think to
look.

The *News* tried to play down the Aurora incident in an
editorial, but inadvertently added a touch more authenticity
to the events by reporting ". . . the biggest man in the country today is the pilot of the airship, a mysterious aerial
plunger who had been seen in the heavens for the past ten
days from the Great Lakes to the Gulf of Mexico."

So what did happen to the little man who came out of
the skies in a strange flying machine? It is known that the
farming folk of Aurora offered prayers for him in the
town's small schoolhouse before he was buried. But for
years the townsfolk were staunch in their denial that he
ever existed, and in their reluctance to discuss the happening. As late as 1973, the International UFO Bureau, an
organization of investigators into the paranormal, sought a

court order to exhume the body of the little stranger to answer the mystery once and for all. The motion was defeated after strong objection from the town's cemetery association. But before he died, an old timer J. C. Curley told the investigators how he and his drinking buddies had seen bits of the airship and the dead pilot. He recalled, "It was difficult to say what he looked like, he was all torn up. But we knew for sure that he was real small . . ."

Today if you ask anybody in Aurora abut a three-foot plot of land in the cemetery where even weeds refuse to grow, they'll tell you it's all a big hoax. But then again, they'll also tell you that the stories in the *Dallas Morning News* never existed!

Little men in flying ships, small, bizarre, half-human creatures that lurk on our country lanes. What next? Would you believe a whole horde of strange little humanoids holding an entire family captive in their Kentucky farmhouse?

Invasion of the Little Men

The "Siege of the Suttons" happened on the balmy night of August 21, 1955 near the town of Kelly, Kentucky, entire population 150. The Suttons lived on the outskirts of town in a one-story home which sported a tin roof. The family didn't have the luxury of telephone, television, or radio, though they were equipped with electricity. The Suttons were simple, God-fearing and hardworking folk. Living with the Suttons were relatives from the Lankford family, and Billy Ray Taylor and his wife. In all there were eight adults and three children residing in the house. It was Billy Ray who would figure most prominently in this wildest of encounters with the unknown and unexplained.

Billy Ray had gone into the backyard for a drink of water when he suddenly burst back into the house, yelling that he'd seen a strange flying object. There was a new

moon on the horizon, and a crystal clear sky, and Billy Ray
was swearing blind that what he saw was a silver flying
saucer spewing out flames. Nobody even bothered to lis-
ten—not even when Billy Ray said it had flown overhead
and then dropped vertically down into a hollow only 300
feet or so behind the Sutton homestead. So much for Billy
Ray's vivid imagination.

Here, however, the tale begins to change from the bizarre to the downright unholy.

At around eight P.M., the Sutton family dog began to
howl uncontrollably, then ran whimpering into a corner.
Lucky Sutton, the hardheaded patriarch of the clan,
thought he saw a strange, glowing orb moving toward the
house. Billy Ray then joined the older Sutton and both of
them, peering out of the window, saw that the strange light
was emanating from what appeared to be a little man about
three-and-a-half feet tall.

When recounting this eerie sight later to sheriff's deputies, both men agreed that the little man had huge saucer
eyes without eyelids or lashes, and large, pointed ears. The
creature's skin was shiny and seemed, at times, to glow,
especially if he went into the shadows around the house.
They said he possessed an abnormally large head with a
small body and scrawny arms and legs. He had long
fingers. Neither could recall having seen any feature identifiable as a mouth or nose. (Recall how remarkably similar
this description is to the Dover Demon?)

Although versions of what exactly happened next at the
Sutton home vary slightly, all agree on the following chro-
nology.

Terrified at what they had seen, Lucky and Billy Ray
grabbed their guns and marched for the door. Lucky carried
a 20-gauge shotgun, and Billy Ray a .22 rifle. When they
were less than twenty feet away from the little man, they
opened fire with a vengeance. What happened next completely boggles the mind. As a hail of bullets and shot hit

the creature, Lucky and Billy Ray watched, stunned, as it simply flipped over backwards and then scurried away into the undergrowth, apparently unharmed.

The two men hot-footed it to the safety of the house. In true horror movie tradition, they were soon to be confronted by the little man's face appearing eerily at the window. This time the terrified men blasted right through the window screen. Once more the creature did a backflip and disappeared without injury into the darkness.

Now the women of the house began to scream. It was obvious things were getting way out of hand. To try and reassure their femalefolk, Lucky and Billy Ray decided to put on a brave face and go out and bring back a body to prove that all was indeed well, and there was no cause for fear. Incredibly, the most bizarre events were yet to come into play.

Billy Ray edged nervously out to the screen door of the porch at the rear of the house, followed closely by Lucky and the rest of the clan. As Billy Ray ventured through the doorway, a clawlike hand reached down from the low roof and viciously grabbed hold of Billy Ray's hair. The totally terrified farmer howled and yanked himself free, as Lucky Sutton burst through the door, blasting wildly chamber after chamber of shot at the little man on the roof. Awestruck, Lucky watched in disbelief as the little man fell off the roof and gently floated to the ground.

This was too much for the family to take. The women were now cowering tearfully behind windows, and the children were sobbing at their skirts.

Suddenly there appeared *another* little man, this one perched in a nearby tree. Billy Ray rushed forth, pumping every bullet he could muster into the creature. This one, too, floated down to the ground. Pandemonium erupted. There were now little men all over the place. Lucky and Billy Ray stood back-to-back, showering bullets and shot in a circle. And each time one of the little people appeared to be hit, he would begin to emanate a strange, bright glow for a second or two. The two men began to back off, carefully retracing their steps toward the house. Just as they were about to back into the door, one of the little men scurried right in front of them.

The seige continued for two more hours. Wave after wave of little men would appear at the windows or could be heard clawing at the door or on the tin roof. By eleven o'clock the Sutton clan was exhausted, their nerves totally frazzled. They decided to make a run for it and abandon the homestead to whatever fate might await it. They crammed themselves into a pickup truck, screamed away from the farm, and headed down US Route 41 to the police department in nearby Hopkinsville.

Struck by the obvious fear displayed by the family and their sincerity, it wasn't long before a posse of state police cruisers were heading for the Sutton property. So convincing was the Sutton clan that, within an hour, the farm was swarming with investigators, the military police from nearby Fort Campbell and, naturally, the media—print, television, and radio.

Their scrounging turned up no evidence of drinking. The Suttons appeared to be the most sober, upstanding family in the community—and they were scared to death. However, not one shred of evidence regarding the visitation of the little people turned up, although there were enough spent cartridges scattered around on the ground to have indicated that something akin to a mini war had taken place. Police Chief Russell Greenweld was quoted as saying, "These people are tough folk, and they are not dumb. Something out here scared them. Whatever it was, it was beyond reason . . . something very weird."

By the early hours of the morning, the last of the investigators and journalists had left empty-handed. But by the doleful, almost pleading, looks on the faces of the Sutton clan as they left, it was pretty obvious to everyone that these frightened folk had experienced something so terrifying, they had been willing to put their reputations at stake in this hard-nosed community.

This book is not intended to prove or disprove these stories, as tall as the tales may seem. There is no intention to logically dissect or analyze them, though an occasional comment or plausible explanation might be offered. The object of this book is to give the facts as they've been recorded and retold, and to let you, the reader, draw your own conclusions.

And we'll have more later about strange, humanlike creatures . . . both little and big.

Welcome to the wonderful world of Bizarre America!

CHAPTER 1

Where in the World...

In Aberdeen, South Dakota, small fish rain from the sky and are seen swimming merrily around in street puddles and water trapped on flat rooftops. In Tarboro, North Carolina, hundreds of fish are found swimming in puddles in tobacco fields after a heavy downpour; and in Providence, Rhode Island, a severe thunderstorm "rains" perch and bullpouts two to three inches long into backyards and on the streets.

In Milwaukee, Wisconsin, the townsfolk are astonished to find their homes covered in huge spider webs which were seen falling from the sky. Workers in a tobacco field in Lebanon, Tennessee, are shocked to find themselves covered in flesh and blood, showering from the sky. In our capital, Washington, D.C., green slime falls from the sky. A shower of live frogs hits Kansas City, Missouri, and in Dubuque, Iowa, tiny frogs are found in hailstones which beat down from the heavens. For three hours it rains beetles over the town of Rock Creek, British Columbia.

The occasional dead bird or two in the street isn't unusual, but when they drop from the sky in flocks, then that's news—even more so when the birds are of multiple species, some of which can't even be identified. Well, it happened in Baton Rouge, Louisiana, where there were so many wild ducks, woodpeckers and catbirds on the streets that they had to remove them with shovels.

In Middleburg, Florida, limestone falls from the sky. So what, you ask. After all those live animals and dead birds, anybody might welcome a bit of limestone dropping into their lives. Except when the limestone in question was a 200-pound block that landed in an open field.

Impossible!

Perhaps these tales of fish, frogs, and cobwebs falling from the heavens are really only the products of overvivid minds? As ludicrous as it sounds, these events really did happen.

They are all a part of Bizarre America.

Our world is full of tales of the impossible and highly improbable. What makes hearing them so fascinating is that they're so unlikely, we find them so extraordinary—and sometimes, so hard to believe. If we saw these wonders with our own eyes, would we perceive them as less fascinating? Probably not. But what if they were happening around us all the time? Wouldn't they perhaps become commonplace? Boring, in fact? If you were to live in Rock Creek and it rained beetles every day, you would; in all likelihood accept such an occurrence as the norm.

This is why we have to put strange phenomena into perspective. What may be strange today could become commonplace tomorrow. But, in the meantime, let's not spoil the fun.

The secret to these tales of the improbable is that they do fall outside our world of the expected. What makes them so special is that they are rarities, the stuff of science fiction. Scientists like to classify these types of baffling phenomena as "transients"—special one-of-a-kind occurrences that aren't duplicated easily, if at all. We all love a mystery, and a true transient is exactly that.

Of course, there can be natural explanations for some illogical events. Various factors can give us a clue to the reasons why something happened. If, say for example, you were a resident of Key West, Florida, and a water spout had been observed at sea, it may not be so surprising to get a downpour of red snapper and bluefish. We could make a good calculated guess that it would be entirely possible for the fish to be caught up in a meandering spout, hurtled around, and held within its grip, possibly even caught up in a coast-bound storm system, and then finally dumped ashore.

So, we say, nothing necessarily unexplainable about fishes falling from the sky. But what if it's out of a clear blue sky, and the fall is over Reno, Nevada, where there isn't even a remote possibility of a nearby, indigenous saltwater fish? That's why we have to look at each transient objectively, with an open mind. If the occurrence fits a logical and explainable, albeit unlikely, pattern, it's not really a mystery. It still might be fantastic, but it's not a true transient.

Let's take the case of the Dover Demon. With so many "reliable" witnesses seeing approximately the same bizarre little man in the same vicinity over a twenty-four-hour period, it would sound most incredulous to say that there *wasn't* anything strange or unusual about this startling event. But how would you view it if I included the fact that a traveling circus playing some three miles away had reported that a young baboon or ape had escaped a couple of days earlier? You might think again, right? It is a historical fact that escaped animals from circuses or zoos have led to outrageous stories involving everything from paranormal animals or humanlike creatures being spotted, to full-blown Bigfoot sightings. Let me add this assurance, though; at the time of the Dover Monster sightings, there were no reports of escaped beasts, large or small, or any other animals on the loose that might have corresponded with the eyewitness sightings.

How about the little man in his flying machine who crash-landed in Aurora. In this day and age it might not be so bizarre to expect a highly sophisticated flying machine to lose control and crash. It also may not be too surprising to find a tiny, mangled body in the wreckage. When people have been blown out of airplanes, whether by terrorist bombs or machine failure or some other form of mishap, it's astounding how well-compacted their bodies become when they hit the ground. Cases are known of skydivers whose parachutes have failed to open who've hit the ground in an upright position. The impact can concertina the body of a six-foot man into that of a two to three-foot midget, while upper chest and facial features can remain pretty much intact. When test pilots or combat fliers come down with their supersonic crafts, it's expected that there will be very little of the pilot's body left to recover.

The evidence from Aurora suggests that there really wasn't too much of the mangled little man left to bury, and we know that high-velocity impact can do strange things to the human body. But remember, in this case, the incident in question happened in 1897. So the chances of these modern-day scenarios applying are not only highly remote, but out of the question. It just goes to show, however, that things may not always be as they initially seem. It's important to entertain all possible, plausible explanations. We all know that forty years ago it would have been impossible to take seriously the thought that men from earth would one day walk on the moon; only a privileged few were privy to the real potential of the rocket engine. Technological miracles can put an entirely new perspective on events that were originally perceived as mysteries. As proof of this, I always like to tell the story of my investigation of a rash of UFO sightings that plagued residents in an area around the

Wright-Patterson Air Force Base during the early seventies.

A UFO or NO?

For weeks, reports had come in from the Dayton, Ohio area of UFOs buzzing rural farmlands. Most of the eyewitness accounts fit the parameters for classic UFO sightings: the crafts were covered with lights and were seen to shine high-intensity beams down from the sky; they were able to accelerate at tremendously high speeds, stop on a dime, and turn in midair; they could drop vertically out of the sky, or rise up from the ground without any forward motion; and, most unbelievably, they could hover, stationary, in midair, move backwards or forwards, and then suddenly take off in any direction at astounding speed.

Helicopters, maybe? No, the eyewitnesses, who always viewed these craft at night, swore that they would recognize the outline of a helicopter and especially the familiar "beating" sound of the rotors. The strange craft they had observed made a noise that came straight from hell; a deafening, thunderous roar, and, from what looked like engine pods or ports, they belched flame. There didn't appear to be any wings or rotor blades.

The accounts were numerous and explicit; anyone reading them would be hard pressed not to believe that these folk were witnessing a genuine invasion of UFOs. Even the local cops could offer no logical explanation. A true mystery, no doubt. Only after days of collecting case histories from fearsome and sometimes irate locals, did something slowly dawn on me. There was very possibly a logical solution, and I thought I knew what it was.

A highly placed contact in the military provided me with the clue I had been looking for. Although it's never been officially admitted, I do believe the Air Force fliers were conducting secret, night-time tests of a new and revolutionary British invention, the Hawker Harrier or—as it was better known—the Harrier Jump-Jet. This super high technology aircraft was later (after successful testing) bought by the U.S. Navy. And in the early seventies, it fit exactly all the parameters of the Dayton sightings.

The Jump-Jet is a VTOL, or vertical take off/landing craft. It has two powerful (and ferociously noisy) Rolls Royce engines, which pivot to allow the aircraft to hover, move forward—or even backwards. Its ideal use is for quick strike operations in inaccessible or built-up areas, such as jungles or even city streets, where runway landing space is unavailable. The Harrier could literally park on a busy Manhattan street. It's also highly successful for aircraft carrier use. There's no doubt in my mind that what was originally perceived as UFO activity were precommission military testings.

It seems then that the events in Dayton were not transients, since there is an explanation—no matter how out of the ordinary it may seem. However, in Aurora, on an April day in 1897, we know for certain that none of these technological advances came into play. And even after all the circumstances are considered, the little man in his flying machine remains as much a puzzle today as it ever was—a true transient.

It will become apparent as we delve further into the world of the unexplained that true transient events are only those that boggle the mind. They have to provoke the response, "That's impossible!" Any logical explanation, whether it be glaringly obvious or quietly oblique immediately robs an event of its aura of mystery.

When all is said and done, this does not mean we will exclude from this book the many quirks of nature. Although not supernatural in the commonly accepted sense of the term, or true transients, they are still events of "supernature," and in themselves they are awe-inspiring, absorbing, mysterious, thought-provoking and, quite frankly, totally fascinating.

Even the wrath of Mother Nature—phenomena such as tornadoes, earthquakes, and lightning, all of which we accept and take for granted—can have a peculiar twist that puts it into the category of the bizarre. For a horse to be swept up and carried away by a tornado is nothing to gasp about (unless you are the unfortunate owner of the animal), but for it to be set down completely unharmed twenty miles away is another matter.

Snowstorms happen as a matter of course in much of the U.S.—but when snowflakes the size of dinner plates come down, now that's bizarre. Hailstones are nothing new, but when they weigh eighty pounds or are the size of golf balls, explode on impact, or are found to contain little creatures, that's news. What would you think of blue-colored rain, or solid chunks of rock that contain live animals? Obviously if something goes totally contrary to the norm, no matter how well accepted the original phenomenon may have been, and under the best of circumstances this diversion from the accepted cannot be repeated, then it falls into the realms of the freaky.

Another factor must also be taken into account when dealing with the bizarre. Out-of-the-ordinary but not totally unusual scenarios may take on an entirely different perspective if they are linked with a peculiar set of circumstances. An earthquake is an unwanted but accepted fact of nature, but consider this scenario that happened in 1886: On August 20, a small comet was spotted crossing the skies. For the next eight days, rock and ashes fell to the ground in the Charleston, South Carolina area. Another "interesting" but "so what?" event.

Not so. On August 31, just eleven days after the comet and the strange showers, Charleston was leveled, completely demolished, by the largest earthquake ever recorded for that area!

Fortean Events

Transient happenings, those that don't fit into the general pattern of things, are often referred to as Fortean Events. The man after whom the term Fortean phenomena was coined is the late Charles Fort—a person who many acknowledge was somewhat eccentric, and some say was just plain nuts.

Charles Fort may best be described today as a pseudo-scientist. A layman by profession, he devoted a great chunk of his life to tracking down and cataloging the bizarre and infamous across the world. It is thanks to the works of Fort—*The Book of the Damned, Lo!, Wild Talents,* and *New Lands*—that we have today one of the best compendiums of unnatural oddities ever compiled.

Fort was almost maniacal in his search for the truth, spending twenty-seven years and thousands of hours poring over newspapers, obscure periodicals, and scientific journals in the New York City Library, The British Museum, and just about any library, big or small, near or remote, that would provide the wacky and offbeat quirks of nature he thirsted for.

Fort was born in Albany, New York, in 1874, and died in the Bronx on May 3, 1932, surrounded by newspaper clippings and manuscripts as he wrestled to the very end to make some common sense out of our uncommon world.

In his own way, Fort was a strange genius who pursued the unnatural with a passion and fervor for the bizarre that was simply not seen in his day. It was very un-chic in scientific circles to so seriously pursue the darker mysteries of life. But today there are many scientists who praise Fort for helping to raise our level of consciousness to recognize and appreciate the absurd that may take place around us.

The following is an apt quote from the cover of *The*

Complete Books of Charles Fort (the latest edition of his works put out by the Dover publishing company), which serves as a tribute to Fort's uniqueness:

> *Charles Fort himself never really explained his phenomena, beyond making vague hints of an organic universe and neo-Hegelianism, yet through the years his following has grown. At first his work was picked up by literary men who admired his gifts greatly, men like Theodore Dreiser, Booth Tarkington, Clarence Darrow, Havelock Ellis, and Oliver Wendell Holmes. Then it influenced the development of science fiction, offering what are called "Fortean Themes." Today it is of triple value, as the great predecessor to all extraterrestrial speculations, far superior in quality to its successors, as a codified source for a multitude of phenomena not readily findable elsewhere, and as a stimulating, bewildering, intoxicating, intellectual tour de force, brilliantly expressed, sometimes convincing.*

If anything, the writings—or as been said more than once, the ramblings—of Charles Fort can be confusing. Fort had a choppy style all of his own, and at times his message can get confusing. One thing that can certainly hold back the neophyte student of Fort is his penmanship; his books are not easy to get into. The flow is disjointed, and the pontificating leads one to think Fort is preaching in a mighty voice. But, once you can learn to appreciate and run with the wide lyric swings and shifts in dialogue, the books become a carnival of the absurd: *The Book of the Damned, Lo!, Wild Talents,* and *New Lands* (more than 1,100 pages in total) are the freakiest fairground sideshow and the Big Top rolled into one.

Where else in the world would you find gathered together such a wild array as: flat earth phenomena; disruptions of gravity; flying machines seen in the sky before the advent of the aircraft; poltergeist phenomena; stigmata; falls of red snow; showers of frogs, fishes, worms, jellies, shells, beetles; infra-Mercurian planets; discrepancies in the schedules of comets; odd phenomena linked to the moon and Mars; the Jersey Devil; strange noises in the sky; teleportation and psychokinesis; unearthly animals and strange beings; unexplained footprints in fresh-fallen snow; spontaneous human combustion . . . the list goes on!

Charles Fort was a scientific revolutionary; he ventured where many men feared to tread. What science sneered at and discounted as spurious or "unscientific," Fort attempted to catalog, to quantify, to put into some semblance of order.

There is a very good reason for my lauding Fort in this book—for without his works stirring this author's interest, there would be no title *Bizarre America*.

CHAPTER 2

Showers That Shouldn't Be

It's November 13, 1833, in Rahway, New Jersey. The most incredible meteor shower ever observed in the United States is taking place over the Eastern Seaboard. Fiery rain is seen coming from the sky. But witnesses, after closer examination, report finding only lumps of jelly on the ground.

On the same day in nearby Newark, a newspaper reports "A mass of gelatinous matter, like soft soap, was found after the great meteor shower. Force of impact disturbed the ground. Substance evaporated readily when heat was applied."

And not too far away in West Point, New York, a woman reports seeing a "round, flattened mass, the size of a coffee cup" fall from the sky. The substance appeared to be transparent, and "quickly evaporated."

On an unknown date in Lowell, Massachusetts, a man was reported to have observed a brilliant shooting star fall to earth some distance from where he was standing. On inspecting the fallen object, he discovered "a jellylike mass" with "an offending smell."

On November 11, 1846, a strangely similar occurrence took place. According to published accounts, ". . . the most remarkable meteor ever seen in this section made its appearance from the west. It appeared larger than the sun, illuminated the hemisphere nearly as light as day. It was in sight nearly five minutes and was witnessed by a great number of inhabitants of the village, and finally fell in a field in the vicinity, and a large company of citizens immediately repaired to the spot and found a body of fetid jelly, four feet in diameter."

In Loweville, New York, also on November 11, 1846, a rather remarkable meteor was seen crossing the heavens. It appeared larger than the sun and illuminated the entire area "nearly as light as day." Many inhabitants of the village claimed to have seen the wonder, which was said to have lasted some five minutes or more in the sky. Then it plummeted to earth, its final resting place in a field on the outskirts of Loweville. According to reports at the time, the local citizenry immediately rushed, en masse, to the spot, only to be disappointed to discover a large body of "fetid jelly," approximately four feet in diameter.

Stone Falls

Not everything that falls from the sky is claimed to be organic in origin. There are many instances of solid rock falls. For the true heavyweights of fall phenomena, nothing quite beats rocks and ice.

Although the block of limestone that fell out of the sky and into a field in Middleburg, Florida, in 1888 would create a mass-media circus of heroic proportions today, surprisingly little has ever been written or published about it—possibly because it's so hard to take it seriously.

The limestone block weighed in at close to 200 pounds. What gives the Middleburg incident credence is that it was written up in the March 9, 1888, issue of *Science,* and the article went on to add that the massive block was put on display at the Sub-tropical Exposition in Jacksonville,

Florida. Whatever happened to the block afterwards has, unfortunately, been lost to antiquity.

While the *Science* article was a serious attempt to record the phenomenon for posterity, the writer did take a somewhat tongue-in-cheek attitude about the whole scene, implying that one moment someone saw something fall from the sky, and the next moment saw a 200-pound block of limestone that had "appeared"—almost miraculously—in "an old, cultivated" field. The writer makes quite clear the insinuation that the block obviously "had been upon the ground in the first place," and was previously unnoticed because it was *so* much a familiar part of the landscape. He suggested that it was only by coincidence—seeing an object fall and then noticing the 200-pound block—that a cause and effect connection had been made.

When analyzing this incident and the rationale in *Science,* Charles Fort took exception to the writer's cavalier attitude. His comments are worth repeating: "The writer who tells us this, with the usual exclusion-imagination known as stupidity, but unjustly, because there is no real stupidity, thinks he can think of a good-sized stone that had for many years been in a cultivated field, but that had never been seen before—had never interfered with plowing, for instance.

"He is earnest and unjarred when he writes that this stone weighs 200 pounds. My own notion, founded upon my own experiences in seeing, is that a block of stone weighing 500 pounds might be in one's parlor twenty years, virtually unseen—but not in an old, cultivated field, where it interfered with plowing—not anywhere—if it interfered."

Thunderstones and Ashes

The term thunderstone has been used for centuries to identify stones which, for some unknown reason, fall during
heavy thunderstorms. Although thunderstones are far from
common, and most instances come from Europe and England, they have been recorded in the United States. The
following is one rare example:

In Richland, South Carolina, in the summer of 1846, a
stone, almost perfectly round and weighing over six
ounces, fell during a violent thunderstorm. The exterior
was coated with a reddish brown glaze, and the interior
was like firebrick.

There is also a strange incident that happened off the
coast of Cape Cod in 1681 which offers a bizarre twist on
the thunderstone theme. According to chroniclers of the
day, the English ship the *Albemarle* was weathering a severe thunderstorm off the Cape. Following a flash of lightning, "a burning, bituminous matter" fell into the stern of
the boat. The odor of the strange substance was similar to
that of gunpowder, and it began to set fire to everything it
touched. "It was in vain that they attempted to extinguish
it with water, and to sweep it overboard with a broom," it
was written at the time.

On the day of June 17, 1857, something similar may
have fallen over Ottawa, Illinois. This time the fall took
the form of hot cinders that "hissed" as they fell from the
sky. According to observers at the time, the weather had
been showery, but nobody heard thunder or saw any lightning. The cinders were described as coming from a north-
easterly direction and were clearly visible as they
approached because they were seen to make a "V" formation in the sky.

Here is one eyewitness account from an Ottawa resident:

"There appeared to be a small, dense cloud hanging over the garden in a westerly direction, or a little to the south of west. The cinders fell upon a slight angle within about three rods [an antiquated measurement of distance] of where I was at work; there was no wind at the moment or none perceptible. My attention was called first to the freak movements in the grass, the next moment to a hissing noise caused by the cinders passing through the air. The larger ones were considerably imbedded in the earth, so much as only to show a small part of it, while the smaller ones were about half buried. I noticed at the time that the ground where I afterwards picked up the cinders showed signs of warmth, as there was quite a steam or fog at that particular point."

Our narrator was clearly impressed by the fact that the cinders were not just hot, but they were hot enough to raise steam from the damp ground where they landed. The narrator was obviously an intelligent or learned soul because not only did he describe the black cinders as "glassy with a cellular interior" but he also differentiated them from meteoric rock because of that internal cellular structure. And he added, "The black cloud, however, resembles those frequently seen in the vicinity of descending meteors."

We usually expect coal to be brought from the depths of the earth—but that's not the way it happened in Springfield, Missouri, on March 2, 1940. That was the day that everyone could keep the home fires burning with coal that fell from the sky.

This oddity took place immediately after a hailstorm. One unidentified chronicler tells the story of a Mr. R.F. Buchanan, who insisted on bringing samples of the coal that had fallen on and around his home at 808 Douglas Street in Springfield. From the account that follows, it seems clear that the coal samples came prepackaged inside the hailstones. The narrator continues: "He [Mr. Buchanan] arrived shortly, but the hail had melted before he got here. He showed me his car, which he had just finished washing previous to the storm. It was literally covered with small pieces of coal, varying from one-sixteenth to one-eighth of an inch cube size. Each little piece of coal was encased in a small, muddy circle on his car, where the hail had melted.

"There were thousands of them on the car top and surface. He said that each hailstone was black in the center before it melted. His lawn, sidewalk, and the street in his section of the city were covered with the bits of 'coal' while several blocks away others advised me that they had noticed the same thing, only it was a mostly black dust deposit after the rain. In all other sections of the city, the deposit was a yellow dust."

While there appears to be no correlation between lumps of coal and a fine yellow dust, the narrator offered his own explanation for the incident—a small tornado might have carried the coal from strip mines a hundred miles away. Perhaps.

And in Pelham, New Hampshire, it did rain that rarest of unearthly rocks, meteors, in 1885—but only in dust form. According to newspaper accounts at the time, sidewalks in the town were covered with metallic dust and granules, positively identified as meteoric in origin, after a sudden thundershower.

The Iceman Cometh

What's the difference between a hailstone and a chunk of ice falling from the sky? The answer, simply, is size. While hailstones have not been recorded as weighing any more than two pounds and never having a diameter larger than five inches, actual ice falls have been known to produce blocks weighing upwards of fifty pounds.

It could be assumed that falling ice is just an extension of the hailstone phenomena; i.e. ice falls are simply larger than normal hailstones. Well, this just doesn't quite follow. When given the strength of vertical winds usually associated with hailstorms, the atmospheric pressure certainly wouldn't be strong enough to hold a forty or fifty pound block of ice suspended in the air. And one must remember that regular-sized hailstones fall to the ground because of one simple fact—they become too heavy to exist in the atmosphere during the prevailing conditions.

Hailstones may collect a little more girth through moisture picked up during their fall to earth, but to imagine that one pea-sized hailstone could attract as much as an additional fifty pounds of ice during its extremely brief descent from the heavens is stretching the imagination. It would appear obvious that ice falls are a totally different animal from regular hailstone showers.

There is another logical explanation for large falling masses of ice—air transportation. It is a certainty that aircraft can accumulate masses of ice on their metallic surfaces. That ice can, and does, break away and fall to earth on occasion. We know all too well from the aftermath inquiries of the Challenger Space Shuttle disaster that potentially hazardous (both to the craft and its occupants and, presumably, to those who may be underneath it) ice can build up when a space vehicle sits on the ground during freezing conditions. Take the following case in point:

*December 13, 1973, Fort Pierce, Florida. An ice chunk roughly ten inches in diameter fell through the roof of a house almost simultaneous with the launch of a Titan 3-C rocket from Cape Canaveral. Chemical analysis showed an unusual concentration of heavy metals within the formation of the ice. Since the rocket trajectory was out over the Atlantic rather than Fort Pierce, it was suggested that the chunk came from an aircraft passing overhead.

But one simple fact remains—many thoroughly reliable accounts of large ice falls were recorded long before man and his flying machines merged into the heavens.

One explanation which is now gaining increasing credibility among meteorologists is that heavy ice chunks falling from the sky may indeed be "visitors" from outer space, space nomads, possibly from galaxies light years away. This begins to make even more sense considering that the latest tests and probes of Halley's Comet when it passed nearby in 1986 confirmed beyond doubt that the comet is not a solid "rocky" piece of intergalactic junk, as was once supposed, but an enormous mass of ice—a giant, dirty snowball of truly cosmic proportions.

This was the overriding theory concerning a large ice fall over Oklahoma:

*March, 1982. Tecumseh, Oklahoma. An ice mass estimated at thirty pounds fell on the land of A.C. Hinson. Investigating meteorologists said that it was not a hailstone, but might have fallen from an airplane or even come from outer space.

For sheer weight and size, however, nothing can touch the chunk of ice that fell on Salina, Kansas, in 1882. It weighed eighty pounds! We can be pretty sure that it didn't fall from a passing airplane. Other record falls include: Woods Cross, Utah, February, 1965; a fifty-pound ice mass fell through the roof of the Phillips Petroleum Plant. Toccoa, Washington, 1959; a thirty-pound ice chunk hurtled out of the sky. Los Angeles, California, January, 1955; large chunks of ice fell, weighing between six and twenty-six pounds. And in Long Beach, California on June 4, 1953, some fifty chunks of ice fell from the sky. Total haul—about a ton of ice!

Back in 1881, a ball of ice measured at a circumference of twenty-one inches fell in Iowa. On January 26, 1958, in San Rafael, California, a slab of ice two-feet square and several inches thick fell through the roof of a house. On September 8, 1958, in Chester, Pennsylvania, a large chunk of ice crashed through the roof of a warehouse. In Aptos, California, in February of 1965 (the same month Phillips Petroleum was hit), a foot-long chunk of ice fell on a home.

There have also been some close shaves from ice falls. But on March 7, 1976, in Timberville, Virginia, three separate blocks of ice apparently fell from the heavens, putting life and limb at risk.

One Wilbert W. Cullers and two friends were sitting comfortably watching TV when, at approximately 8:45 P.M., they heard a deafening crash which made the house tremble. A block of ice the size of a basketball came through the tin roof of the home, smashed through a two-by-four joist, hit the floor below, and barreled on through the plasterboard ceiling to land in the room below, narrowly missing Cullers and his friends. The astonished men, not knowing what to make of the sudden attack, called the sheriff's department.

When deputies from Rockingham County arrived about an hour later, they found no injuries, just a three-gallon bucket in which the men had saved the fragments of the ice bomb. It was described as "murky" ice, and Sergeant C.R. Hottinger was reported as saying the ice was "milky white, cold, and compressible in the hand."

On investigation, the deputies were to discover that not far away a neighbor, John Branner, was in his driveway when he heard the impact of the ice block hitting the Cullers's home. Young Cindy Lewis, a fifteen-year-old living across from the Cullers's residence, heard the impact and rushed out, expecting to find a car crash. She said she heard a "whizzing" sound, looked up, and witnessed another block of ice smash into the roadway nearby. John Branner also witnessed this same missile hit the earth but from a vantage point some fifty yards away. Branner could not remember any sound accompanying the fall, but he did look up and note that he could see no aircraft in the sky.

The next morning on Monday, March 8, Laurence Cline, who owned a farm a mile west of Timberville, went out to feed his chickens and found a large block of ice on the ground.

Later examination of particles from the Timberville ice falls were analyzed at Eastern Mennonite College, where it was discovered that the ice was composed of water very similar to local tap water, and contained yeastlike organisms and bacteria. One small fragment of gravel was also discovered, although it could not be positively proven that this had not been collected with the samples, rather than having been imbedded in them.

It was noted at the time of the Timberville incidents that weather conditions would have made it very unlikely for such large chunks to accumulate on an aircraft. But that does not account for the fact that the aircraft may have passed through some far distant frigid atmosphere and built up sizable ice deposits, which then melted in a warmer atmosphere and were deposited on Timberville.

During the month of May, 1957, in Forked River, New Jersey, Robert Cloupe and his son Robbie were out in their garden planting some vegetables. It was an overcast Memorial Day when they were startled by a whistling sound in the sky. The sound—"like a firecracker makes before it explodes," Mr. Cloupe said—occurred around 3:45 P.M. Robbie told his father to look above them, and together they observed "something" fall into a field next to their neighbor's house a short distance away. The object, they discovered, was apparently an ice ball. Having left a six-inch deep impression in the ground where it landed, the main mass had then broken up into "grapefruit-sized chunks," six to eight inches in diameter, which were spread over an area some twenty-five feet across.

And then there is the case of Dr. Botts. On September 11, 1949, in Stephen County, Texas, Dr. Robert Botts was nearly beaned by a forty-pound chunk of ice that landed at his feet out of a clear blue sky.

In Reading, Pennsylvania, on July 30, 1957, a man and his wife narrowly escaped being hit by a chunk of ice two feet in diameter which fell next to them.

A one-foot long chunk of ice fell next to a child playing outside her home in Buffalo, New York, on September 11, 1959.

And on February 5, 1968, in our nation's capital, Washington D.C., a ball of ice seven to eight inches in diameter crashed through the awning outside a store on a busy city street.

Weaving a Web of Intrigue

The good folk of Milwaukee, Wisconsin, were the first to provide an accurate and concise report of web-falls in the United States. The year was 1881, and the month, October. To awake one morning and find your home and street covered in spiderlike webs, is not everybody's idea of an idyllic fall—snow, maybe; spider webs, definitely not.

These sleepy-eyed people of Milwaukee may be forgiven for imagining that they were still in the grips of some horrific nightmare.

The few witnesses who actually saw the webs falling said that they "came from a great height." In fact, they were seen "as far up in the air as the power of the eye could reach." The strands were described as ranging from two feet in length to many yards. In all cases the webs were very strong in texture and a bright white in color.

In nearby Green Bay, residents experienced a similar fall. The only difference was, the webs, that seemed to come from the direction of the bay, ranged in size from mere specks to a maximum of sixty feet. Residents in Vesburg, Fort Howard, Sheboygan, and Ozaukee, all reported web-falls in their areas.

And out of all the eyewitness accounts, not one attested to the presence of a single spider!

Falls of gossamer from the sky are not at all unusual. Because of an almost lighter than air characteristic, gossamer, or spiders' webs, can easily travel great distances on the lightest of breezes. Who hasn't at some time experienced a spider's web traveling like a will-o'-the-wisp on the wind. But when prodigious webs fall from great heights in quantities that defy nature, then we have a genuine phenomena.

Web-falls have been recorded in long strands, tangled sheets, and even as giant balls. In some instances observers have noted that the webs are tough, elastic, and often hard to break. In some areas, notably Wisconsin, the falls of weblike material have covered hundreds of square miles. But who makes these webs, and where do they come from? One thing is certain: rarely, if not at all, are spiders ever found in them.

Take the following report, with a little help from the friendly postmaster at Gainsville, Florida, as typical:

*September 20, 1892. Southeastern United States. "The postmaster of Gainsville, Florida, writes as follows: 'I enclose you something which has created a great deal of curiosity in our community; it was first discovered late this afternoon floating in the air or falling from the clouds. I have seen people, who live at least ten miles apart, who tell the same story—that it sometimes falls in long strands like spider webs, two to three-thousand yards long, then doubled up into strands and wads.' The following letter, written by a correspondent from Gainsville, Florida, to our fellow-member Judge L.C. Johnson, of Meridian, Mississippi, refers to the same phenomenon. This letter is dated September 21, 1892. 'Of all the curious things in nature the inclosed [sic] webs are among the strangest. Yesterday great white sheets were seen floating with the daily showers, resembling large, pure white spider webs, some of them fifty yards or more in length. The trees in many cases are covered. Near the small stream, about 100 yards from the house, some of it extended as an immense web; in other places it rolled up into a ball.' "

Another curious factor associated with web-falls is that the substance itself may evaporate or disappear as soon as it is handled or touches the ground. Two reports, one from Montreal, Quebec, and the other from St. Louis, Missouri, both fit this category.

*October 10, 1962. Montreal, Quebec. "At 20:00 GMT while the *Roxburgh Castle* was moored at her berth in Montreal, I was walking around outside my accommodation and noticed fine white filaments of unknown kind hanging around stanchions and topping lift wires of derricks. Calling the attention of the Chief Officer, I pulled one of these strands from a stanchion and found it was quite tough and resilient. I stretched it, but it would not break easily (as, for instance, a cobweb would have done) and after keeping it in my hand for three or four minutes it disappeared completely; in other words it just vanished into nothing. Looking up, we could see small cocoons of the material floating down from the sky but as far as we could ascertain, there was nothing either above or at street level to account for this extraordinary occurrence."

*October, 1969. St. Louis, Missouri. "Great globs of spider-weblike material descended from the sky, alarming numerous citizens. As Donald Pecsok, director of the county's air pollution control division, remembers, hundreds of calls poured into the newspapers and his office. People thought the material was from an exploded test airplane from the nearby McDonnell Douglas plant; thought it was from a flying saucer; or thought it was a divine sign, etc. According to nearby rural residents, says Pecsok, the globs contained a few eggs of 'balloon spiders,' which spun the material at the tops of trees and left it there for the wind to catch. Unfortunately, most of the material dissolved as it hit the ground. Some that was retained and put under a microscope resembled a spider web, but Pecsok is reluctant to make any great claims because he could not get any local scientist to investigate . . . Although the event is listed as a 'spider invasion,' Pecsok notes that he found only one spider, a small brownish creature, about an eighth of an inch in diameter and about the size of a quarter with its legs stretched out (apparently very dead)."

The latest twist to be added to the phenomena of falling webs is a UFO connection. For some unexplained reason there have been a number of reported sightings of Unidentified Flying Objects during which gossamerlike substances were seen.

On October 11, 1950, a report came from Butte, California that the sky was filled with hundreds of speeding silvery white balls heading north. They were said to be easily seen dividing, uniting, or disappearing altogether. Each of the little balls was described as about the size of a dinner plate. Whether these little balls were indeed some form of strange craft (certainly they *were* unidentified flying objects, though perhaps not in the strictest sense) or an airborne artifact of nature is open to debate. The very next day a tree was discovered covered with a mass of unexplainable gossamer.

But in September of 1948, a more tangible eyewitness account from Ontario, was hard to ignore:

*September 26, 1948. Port Hope, Ontario. "This day was warm and the sky cloudless. We had dinner [persons of English origin often refer to lunch as dinner and dinner as supper—author's note] in the garden and I was lying on my back on the lawn, my head just in the shade of the house, when I was startled to see an object resembling a star moving rapidly across the sky. The time was two o'clock, Eastern Standard Time.

"At first it was easy to imagine that the recent reports of 'Flying Saucers' had not been exaggerated. More of these objects came sailing into view over the ridge of the house, only to disappear when nearly overhead. With field glasses I was able to see that each was approximately spherical, the center being rather brighter than the edges. The glasses also showed quite a number at such heights that they were invisible to the naked eye.

"With only a gull flying in the sky for comparison, I should estimate the elevation of the lower objects to be about 300 feet, and the higher ones 2,000 feet; the size was about one foot in diameter, and the speed about thirty mph, in a direction SW to NE. Also visible now and then were long threads, apparently from spiders. Some of these were seen to reflect the light over a length of three or four yards, but any one piece may of course have been longer. Each was more or less horizontal, moving at right angles to its length. In one case an elongated tangled mass of these gave the appearance of a frayed silken cord. These threads appeared only in the lower levels [or were not visible at higher altitudes—author's note]."

* * *

From thousands of yards of gossamer on the ground to webs flying along in the air with UFOs. There is but one hope as far as these gigantic weblike structures go—that there aren't any gigantic spiders coming along with them!

Miscellaneous Falls

Into every life must fall a bit of rain, or so the saying goes. And so it should follow that out of every series of bizarre falls there are some so unique that they don't fit into any recognizable category. We will be dealing with animal falls, possibly the strangest of all fall categories, in the following chapter. The tail end of this chapter is devoted to a small selection of those falls that are so weird, or one-of-a-kind that they don't fit any recognizable pattern.

For example, on September 5 and 6, 1978, Washington, D.C. was inundated by green slime falling from the sky. According to reports at the time, the affected area was generally bound by Rock Creek Parkway on the west, Pennsylvania Avenue (a rather prestigious street, to say the least) on the north, G Street on the south, and Twenty-third Street on the east.

The green ooze was said to have injured plants, killed off small wildlife animals and insects, stripped the paint from automobiles, and smeared windshields—much to the annoyance of drivers. As well as having to cope with angry residents of this area—one such resident complained bitterly that half the flowers in her backyard garden began to wilt and keeled over and died during the two days of the slime shower—the city health officials were totally stymied as to what to make of the green horror.

It was also noted at the time that the substance did surely fall from a great height, as opposed to having been sprayed or deposited on the ground by some other means, because the entire roof of a twelve-story building was completely coated with the offending substance. To this day, nobody has come up with a satisfactory answer to what the substance was or where it came from.

A strange experience happened in Cumberland, Kentucky. Unfortunately, the date of the following first-person account is unknown, although in all likelihood, from the language and descriptions, it could be early nineteenth century:

*"While we were in that land of waterfowl below Cumberland, I witnessed a shower of feathers; as we sailed up a reach of the river with a fresh breeze, without the knowledge of a human being within many miles of us, it appeared to be snowing; this was nothing more than small feathers, and we supposed that at some Indian camp in the swamps to the windward the operation of goose-plucking must be going on; these feathers had likely traveled many miles, and would continue while the breeze lasted."

*In 1850 in Napoleon, Kansas, a sudden rainstorm changed color and substance to a yellow, viscous liquid which left a thick scum on the surface of everything it touched; on March 21, 1898, in Mount Vernon, Kentucky, a substance that looked like liquid sulphur rained from the sky and burned when it hit the ground, giving off sulphurous fumes; on March 12, 1867, in South Union, Kentucky, a yellow substance was recorded as having fallen from the sky like rain; and in Amesbury, Massachusetts and Prospect, New York, on June 18, 1860, the ground was covered with "sulphur" after a thunderstorm. Contemporary reports stated it burned with a blue flame and smelled like common sulphur.

*   *   *

And how about this one from Louisiana:

*Lake Providence, Louisiana (no date given). "It is stated that during a heavy thunderstorm near Lake Providence, a number of small bodies were found on the ground, immediately after the shower, scattered along the shore of the Mississippi River for a distance of forty miles above the lake; as many as half a bushel being collected around one house. These, on being submitted to critical examination, proved to be the scales of the common gar-fish of the South (Lepidosteus). The species inhabits the shallow, muddy waters of the South and sometimes attains a length of five or six feet, and is especially characterized by being enclosed in an almost impenetrable coat of mail (the scales in question), so compact as almost to resist the penetration of a bullet. It is very difficult to give credence to this story; as the gar-fish are not particularly abundant, and the method of aggregation of so large a number of detached scales would be a problem extremely difficult of solution. Perfectly authentic instances are on record of small fish, shells, etc., being taken up in storms and scattered over the earth; but when it comes to portions of fishes which weigh from five to fifty pounds each, the draft upon one's faith is rather too severe."

The author of the latter paragraph may not have been so astounded had he had full knowledge of what follows in our next chapter!

CHAPTER 3

Dr. Graves's Mysterious Glob

There's a wonderful story about a glob of strange matter that fell from the sky over Amhurst, Massachusetts, during the early nineteenth century. The twists and turns the tale takes embodies all the idiosyncracies that surround curious things that rain from the heavens. To add to the authenticity of the whole matter, the ungodly glob was found by no less a person than a retired college lecturer, a professor of chemistry. And the affair was to be discussed in no less a prestigious organ than the *American Journal of Science*. And it didn't escape the attention of Mr. Charles Fort.

Believe it or not, there's also a follow-up story . . . another glob supposedly fell near the same spot years later and was once more "examined by science!"

It all starts with Professor Rufus Graves, former lecturer in chemistry at Dartmouth College. The time is between eight and nine in the evening and the date August 13. We can picture the scholarly professor sitting back in a rocking chair, possibly on the front porch of his small house, and savoring the warm night air as the sun's last glimmers give a faint red cast to the horizon. Suddenly Dr. Graves is jolted out of his mental meanderings by a brilliant flash of white light. As the professor tells it, he observed a fireball in the sky that plunged earthward to land only feet from his house.

Rushing over to the fall site, Graves discovers a strange, dishlike object, round and about eight inches in diameter and one inch thick. It was buff-colored and covered by a downy, velvety substance which Graves referred to as having "a nap similar to milled cloth."

Graves began to carefully peel away the surface to discover that underneath was a pulpy substance that reminded him of the consistency of soft soap. But what astounded the professor most was the incredibly bad smell this substance gave off. "It was an offensive, suffocating smell, producing nausea and giddiness," he was to tell later. Totally perplexed by his find, the good professor was in for another shock.

Within a few minutes of being exposed to the air, the visitor from the sky began to change its color. From the bland buff that it was, the object, as if alive, took on a livid red color. In fact, Graves described it as "resembling venous blood." And then it melted. Whatever the professor had in his hands now, it was clearly a rather putrid and unwholesome sight.

The story was giddily recounted in local ale houses, and the professor became somewhat of a celebrity, if not known as the "Mad Professor" by less understanding wits of the day. Whatever exactly became of the strange red goo has gone unrecorded.

Scientific Credence

However, the affair wasn't to end there but was to take on a more scientific tone when it was written up in the *American Journal of Science*. The account in the *Journal* came from and refers to a Professor Dewey, but there seems little doubt that Professor Dewey and Professor Rufus Graves are one and the same person. It was not unknown for men of science when reporting oddities—for which they might reap ridicule or loss of professional respect—to use a pseudonym as a safety net. The facts as given to the *Journal* are just too close to those of Professor Graves to be mere coincidence. The date is the same, August 13, 1819, and so is the location, Amhurst, although there are some small inconsistencies.

In the *Journal*'s account, Professor Dewey was said to have heard an explosion and seen a falling object. The explosion was intense enough to create a bright light that was reflected on a wall of Professor Dewey's home and was witnessed by other members of his family who were in the house at the time. The next morning the professor found an object in his front yard. It was bowl-shaped, about eight inches in diameter, and one inch thick. "It was bright buff-colored, and having on it a fine nap." The professor also commented, "It was unlike anything before observed by anyone who saw it." He then described how he removed the covering and found a pulpy substance that emitted "an offensive, suffocating smell."

In the final line of the report, Professor Dewey explains that with exposure to the air it changed to "a livid color resembling venous blood" . . . and then the "thing" liquified!

But let's turn our attention to another fascinating case of falling organic matter before returning to the conclusion of Dr. Graves and his gelatinous glob and some possible solutions.

Flying Cows?

It was known as "The Kentucky Phenomenon," and occurred on March 3, 1876. There's only one way of describing what took place . . . chunks of beef began raining from the sky over Olympian Springs, Bath County, Kentucky.

To be more accurate, the beeflike substance was described mostly as being in flake form, each flake varying from about as big as a thumbnail to the size of a large manila envelope. It provided a thick layer covering the ground, trees, and fences. Interestingly the meat shower was localized in one small spot, a strip of land about one hundred yards long and some fifty yards wide. The fall apparently took place out of a clear blue sky and caused such a stir that it was written up in the *New York Times* a week later on March 10, and then a later report appeared in *Scientific American*.

The controversy surrounding the Kentucky fall split the scientific community. That the fall did indeed happen, there is no doubt. Newspapers had columns of quotes from eyewitnesses, and there wasn't the merest hint that the bizarre happening was a hoax. What did confuse the scientists was the attempt to attach a label to the material that resembled animal flesh. Half the investigators were willing to accept that the beef-flakes were indeed that, or at least something organic, most probably animal tissue that had rained from the sky.

The rest of the scientific investigators preferred a rather novel explanation—the material was in fact *nostoc*. But more about nostoc in a moment.

What makes this single fall incident so intriguing is that nobody questioned the fact that the substance fell from the skies. With so many firsthand accounts from folk who were able to look up and see what they believed was a cloud of this stuff, and then witness it floating to earth, the evidence was indisputable. Had there been just one witness, or had somebody stumbled upon the material covering the ground and hanging from the branches of trees, then the believability factor would have been greatly reduced.

There was, however, a well documented incident in Wilson County, Tennessee, which was incredibly similar to the Kentucky fall. But the facts surrounding the event were highly questionable. The *American Journal of Science* was the first to publish details of the strange occurrence. According to its report, a gentleman by the name of Dr. Troost had traveled to Wilson County to investigate the incident which involved chunks of flesh raining down over some tobacco fields—and the unfortunate workers in the fields were spattered with the rotting remains.

Dr. Troost concluded in his *Journal* piece that the substance was "clear blood and portions of flesh." His explanation was that a whirlwind could have picked an animal up in one spot, torn the creature apart during its ferocious travels, and then dumped it over the tobacco fields. But this was not to be so.

On further investigation, the entire escapade was discovered to be a hoax. Three issues later, the *Journal* printed a brief apology and explanation of the Wilson County affair. A group of tobacco field workers, whether to test the gullibility of their bosses or to just plain make monkeys out of them, had invented the whole story of the fall. To add credence to it, they had scattered chunks of rotten flesh from a half-decayed hog around the fields. It was enough "evidence" to take in not only the general populace but to fool at least one noted scientist and the *American Journal of Science*.

Needless to say, with hoaxes like the Wilson County fall, the scientific community was likely to be a little gunshy in the future when it came to pronouncing an incident of fall phenomenon as genuine.

Not So Logical Explanations

So, in Amhurst, Massachusetts and Olympian Springs, Kentucky, we have two cases where the falls were indeed accepted as genuine, but the big problem was identifying the substances.

Was there a logical explanation?

The answer to that question is yes . . . and no!

We briefly referred to nostoc. Nostoc frequently gets tagged by scientists as the most likely culprit in many incidences of falls of unexplainable organic material. But what exactly is nostoc? The dictionary definition of the substance is "any of a genus of blue-green algae, having twisted, coiled filaments embedded in a gelatinous material and forming spherical colonies." Clearly nostoc sounds like it could be a prime candidate for falls of unexplainable jelly or fleshlike materials—and "nostoc" also has a nice, inoffensive ring about it.

But why nostoc should be floating around the sky and not sitting at the bottom of some mill pond is another question the scientists can't readily answer. So much for theories.

There's also the question of nostoc being a bluish to greenish algae. In scientific terms that's the generally accepted color scale associated with nostoc—but, as Charles Fort points out, that doesn't necessarily have to be so. Who is to say that nostoc can't be buff-colored (as in the Amhurst fall) or flesh-colored (as in the Olympian Springs fall)? Comments Fort, "Now, I can't say that nostoc is always greenish, any more than I can say that blackbirds are always black, having seen a white *(albino)* one: we shall quote a scientist who knew of flesh-colored nostoc, when so to know was convenient. When we come to reported falls of gelatinous substances, I'd like it to be noticed how often they are described as whitish or graying. In looking up the subject, myself, I have read only of greenish nostoc."

Fort goes on to cite scientific organs that variously describe nostoc as "blue-green"; "from bright green to olive green"; "green"; and "greenish."

He concludes, "It would seem acceptable that, if many reports of white birds should occur, the birds are not blackbirds, even though there have been white blackbirds. Or that, if often reported, grayish or whitish gelatinous substance is not nostoc, and is not spawn occurring in times unseasonable for spawn."

Which brings us nicely to one scientific offering as an explanation for the Kentucky affair.

The *New York Times* of March 12, 1876 reported that the substance found at Olympian Springs had been examined and analyzed by a man of science identified as Professor Smith. Professor Smith's conclusion was that the flakes of supposed beef flesh were simply the "dried spawn of some reptile, doubtless a frog" which had been picked up in one place and set down in another. Fort takes issue with the term "dried" and points out that by the time Professor Smith received his sample, it may well have been "dried" —very dried—but that doesn't reflect the true condition of the substance as it was picked off the trees and fences in Olympian Springs.

Beware Buzzards!

While nostoc is still the favorite theory of scientists who probed the Kentucky affair, other explanations from the scientific community get even whackier!

According to Dr. A. Mead Edwards, who is described as President of the Newark Scientific Association, in New

Jersey, the substance was examined and indeed was found to be nostoc. But a gentleman by the name of Dr. Hamilton, who also received a sample, was absolutely positive it was . . . lung tissue! To confuse matters even further, a scientist by the name of Dr. Edwards, who was firmly convinced the substance was nostoc until he got a hands-on sample, also declared it to be lung tissue. Dr. Edwards confirms that he wrote to other scientists examining samples from Kentucky and received various reports, mostly agreeing that whatever fell from the sky over Olympian Springs was made up of "cartilage" and "muscle fibers."

So, what's the bottom line? What is one to believe?

Well, here it comes. The officially accepted explanation for the Kentucky Phenomenon was . . . a flock of buzzards!

Many of the scientists went along with this, and certainly the local folk in Olympian Springs agreed it was the most acceptable explanation.

This is how it *really* happened: a flock of extremely hungry buzzards set down on the remains of some dead cow and gorged themselves stupid. Then, after their bullish banquet, the birds took off, only to find themselves too heavy for comfortable flight (or too nauseous from overeating), and promptly disgorged the contents of their stomachs over Olympian Springs!

Possible? Well, plausible at least.

The Mystery of Dr. Graves Solved?

But what about Amhurst and Dr. Graves? The story was to take on a bizarre twist.

According to the *American Journal of Science* a gentleman by the name of Professor Edward Hitchcock was to take up residence in Amhurst some years after the original 1819 fall. And lo and behold, Dr. Graves was once more to be the recipient of fall phenomena! As batty as it sounds,

Professor Hitchcock was invited by Dr. Graves to examine the substance from the second Amhurst fall. By all accounts, the substance was approximately the same size and weight, and a similar buff-colored and nap covered as the original—and Professor Hitchcock was to recognize its true identity immediately!

What Dr. Graves presented him with was, after all, just a common-or-garden fungus. Not content with just identifying the genus of the glob, Professor Hitchcock went on to name the exact species of the fungus (although there is no record of what this was) and to predict that, like wild toadstools and mushrooms, there was every likelihood that more would spring up within the next twenty-four-hour period. Two more *were* found before the very next day, according to contemporary accounts.

The Amhurst fall now seems to make perfect sense. There may well have been a fall over the small Massachusetts town, a bright light descending to earth; but that fall is likely to have been a meteorite (or even a shooting star). The good Professor Graves may be forgiven for confusing the fall (of which there is little doubt that something bright did fall) with the chance happening of discovering at the same time a rather bizarre-looking and smelly fungus near his home. Remember that Dr. Graves peeled off a naplike outer coating from his fleshy, disc-shaped object, and compare this with peeling the sometimes naplike surface coating from particular strains of edible mushrooms. What happened next was that the fungus, as do many of nature's oddball fungi, quickly died and formed a gelatinous, foul smelling glob.

It all fits, doesn't it?

Well, not exactly. There still remains the question of the object turning to a vivid red, the color of venous blood—a fact which Dr. Graves swore vehemently did happen. That part of the mystery we may never be able to solve. And that's probably as well.

Charles Fort sums it up quite succinctly: "We shall have many data of gelatinous substance said to have fallen from the sky: almost always the exclusionists argue that it was only nostoc, an Alga [sic], or, in some respects, a fungous [sic] growth. The rival convention is spawn of frogs or of fishes.

"These two conventions have made a strong combination. In instances where testimony was not convincing that gelatinous matter had been seen to fall, it was said that the gelatinous substance was nostoc, and had been upon the ground in the first place: when the testimony was too good that it had fallen, it was said to be spawn that had been carried from one place to another in a whirlwind."

The astute Mr. Fort quite rightly makes the point that science can eagerly at will alter its explanations to fit the scenario of most unexplained happenings.

What these incidences should tell us is that there may be a number of explanations for showers of organic matter from the heavens, and whichever version you choose to believe, whether it's disgorging buzzards or a coincidental find of exotic fungi, that is entirely up to you—because none has been totally, adequately explained in scientific terms!

So, did Dr. Graves really make a genuine mistake? Did he spot a meteorite and find a strange gelatinous substance and put two and two together and come up with five? Common sense dictates that that's exactly what Dr. Graves did.

Or did he?

The case histories in the next chapter may make you want to think again.

CHAPTER 4

A Catalog of the Curious

You'd think the statistic sheets on strange phenomena might make for dry reading. But the what, where, and how many of Fortean events makes for intriguing reading. And why not! Who wouldn't want to know how many cases of animals falling out of the skies had been reported? Where are UFOs most commonly sighted? Which are the classic "strange" areas of the United States? Where do the most sea serpent reports come from? And how many ghostly poltergeist attacks have ever been recorded?

Considering the many thousands of pieces of information necessary to put together this jigsaw puzzle of the unusual, it would be a daunting task. Yet one man did it.

Fascinating Facts

Back in the early seventies, Dr. Michael Persinger, associate professor of psychology and a research scientist at Laurentian University in Sudbury, Ontario, set about this mission impossible. He combed the works of Charles Fort, scientific journals, newspaper clippings, and speciality magazines to come up with what must be the most comprehensive series of maps ever produced to illustrate the extent of unexplained events across the United States.

After collecting massive amounts of data (6,060 recorded events worldwide), Persinger fed all his material into a computer. What he produced was an astonishing amount of fascinating data.

Persinger classified life's oddities into eleven major categories: fall phenomena, electromagnetic phenomena, unusual sonic (or sound) phenomena, UFO reports, unusual human behavior and properties, unclassified animals, unusual forces, astronomical peculiarities, geophysical oddities, meteorological infrequent events, and strange archaeological finds.

The professor's objective was to see if any patterns evolved across the United States. As was expected, there was a distinct correlation between areas of high population and high numbers of reported unusual events. This makes sense; the more people there are to observe any transient event, the higher the likelihood of reports. As Dr. Persinger states, "Since the human observer has been the primary recorder of this phenomena, the number of unusual and transient events, because of their typical localized manner, should reflect the number of measurement devices (human observers) in the locality." But the scientist did find anomalies. "Significant deviations from population distribution do exist, however, especially in the midwestern portions of the United States," he says.

In other words, in the midwest, where population is lowest, you would expect far fewer, if any, reports of Fortean events. Persinger found that this just wasn't so—even in remote, lowly populated areas of the United States, significant numbers of unusual events are taking place. To my mind this is very telling; it certainly tends to put down the often quoted theory of strange events being attributed to mass hysteria. It also leads us to believe that, despite the causes of these strange ripples in our normally well organized world, the phenomena are less likely to be influenced by man and more likely to be true freaks of nature. To simplify this even further; whatever the mechanics are of bizarre occurrences, man has no control—he is only the observer. And that's what makes Fortean phenomena so fascinating; it is beyond our reach, and, for now, possibly our understanding!

As well as being able to create unusual events maps for the entire United States, Persinger was to make some other interesting findings. He discovered that there were distinct links between certain types of phenomena and, equally significant, no links at all between others. These links don't necessarily mean that different kinds of phenomena usually happen at the same time, for example, falls of frogs from the sky and earthquakes. But in areas where these bizarre events have happened, there have also been significant reports of other strange happenings.

Persinger found that of the eleven main categories of the unusual, he could isolate three distinct groups; three clusters in which different events seem to interrelate or hang together. In the first group those which showed high correlations of incidence were fall phenomena, electromagnetic peculiarities, UFOs, unusual human behavior and properties, unusual forces, and geophysical oddities.

The second group of oddities which stuck together were unclassified animals, meteorological oddities, and strange archaeological finds. Within this group the strongest correlation was between the incidences of sightings of strange animals and the findings of bizarre fossil remains (one which appears to make complete sense). When studying the maps and statistics, what became very apparent was the distinct lack of crossover between events in the first and the second group. There appeared to be little, if no connection between the categories of fall phenomena, electromagnetic peculiarities, UFOs, unusual human behavior, unusual forces, and geophysical oddities and the categories of unclassified animals, meteorological anomalies and strange archaeology.

The odd man out was bizarre sound phenomena. This single category of sonic strangeness did not correlate with any of the other oddball happenings and stood completely alone.

Clearly it helps to give us some insight into Fortean phenomena if we can first recognize which types of events are likely to happen together with, or in the same area, as others. Persinger's work resulted in some valuable clues into the mechanics of Fortean events, even if it wasn't able to explain them. But, then again, if that had happened, we wouldn't have all these wonderful mysteries to ponder.

What in the World...

One of the greatest values of Dr. Persinger's work is that it gives us a feel for how many strange events are happening, what types, and where. We can even identify hot spots of activity.

What follows is a list of some of the most significant findings on Fortean phenomena. It is not a comprehensive catalog of Persinger's scientific findings, for that would take an entire book—as it did in Persinger's work entitled *Space-Time Transients and Unusual Events*. What you will find are selected categories of anomalous phenomena together with some typical examples (many more will be detailed later in this book) to whet the appetite. Call it a primer on the bizarre and unusual.

Fall Phenomena

While anything that falls from the sky that isn't rain, hail, or snow is unusual, fall phenomena literally fall into four main categories: falls of rock, falls of ice, falls of solids, and falls of animals.

As in all examples of bizarre phenomena (and this should be noted for the following categories as well), nobody can say that the figures are absolutely accurate. It would be almost impossible to record every single incidence of animal parts, ice blocks, or toads raining from the sky, or to say with certainty that those recorded are the only incidences. What we can say with some surety is that these are a good reflection of the overall situation.

The total of all strange falls from the sky came to 255 distinct and separate incidents. Among them were thirty-three recordings of rock falls, sixty-six cases of ice falls, ninety-nine instances of solid falls, and fifty-six animal or animal-related falls. Here are some examples:

Rock Falls

*March 1888 in Middleburg, Florida. A block of limestone falls from the sky.

*May, 1874. A rock shower hits Los Angeles.

*June 16, 1884. In Trenton, New Jersey, stones fall in farmer's field.

*July, 1921. Sporadic falls of rocks hit Chico, California. It is recorded to have lasted a week or more.

*July, 1962. Numerous windows are broken in San Bernardino, California, when pebbles rain down.

*June, 1968. Hot rocks fall on Valley Stream, New York. Reports indicate they were still warm to the touch when recovered by local residents.

Ice Falls

*August, 1882. An eighty-pound chunk of ice falls in Salinas, Kansas.

*(month unknown), 1888, Chicago, Illinois. Large clumps of ice drop from the sky. They weigh up to two pounds each.

*(month unknown), 1889. Aitkin, Minnesota, is plunged into sudden darkness followed by large chunks of falling ice.

*January, 1955. Los Angeles is hit by large chunks of ice. Some weigh over thirty pounds.

*September, 1958. A seventy-pound chunk of ice lands in Madison County, New Jersey.

*(month unknown), 1959. In Martin, Georgia, a fifty-pound ice block falls from a clear sky.

Solid Falls

*(month unknown), 1833. Jellylike lumps fall on Nelson County, Virginia.

*(month unknown), 1857. A cotton-candylike substance falls over Clear Lake, California.

*November 16, 1857. In Charleston, South Carolina, large masses of bristling fibers slowly fall from the heavens. The substance is described as "like angel hair."

*(month unknown), 1858. A fused copper-metal object falls in Marblehead, Massachusetts.

*May 11, 1894. In Vicksburg, Mississippi, a large piece of alabaster falls during a hailstorm.

*July 21, 1920. Fragments of china fall during a thunderstorm in Portland, Oregon.

*October 15, 1922. Weblike substances fall on the lake shore near Chicago, Illinois.

*August 16, 1951. A five-pound ball of steel falls in Tacoma, Washington.

*August, 1956. Silver foillike substance rains down over Jackson, California.

*February, 1958. A shower of seeds hits Savannah, Georgia.

*November 25, 1961. Over a ton of polyethylene film drops on Elizabethon, Tennessee.

*July 12, 1961. Peaches fall from a cloudy sky in Shreveport, Louisiana.

*August, 1962. In Blackstone, Virginia, beans and peas rain from the sky during a thunderstorm.

*July 25, 1963. Quantities of corrugated aluminum fall on Cleveland, Ohio.

*July, 1963. Houses in Terre Haute, Indiana, are caked with a mudlike slime which falls from the sky.

*January 22, 1964. Thousands of white beans appear on the ground after a rainfall.

*(month unknown), 1971. Chunks of hay fall from the sky in Springwater, New York.

*September 9, 1972. Tampa, Florida is inundated with a foul smell when a sooty substance rains down.

Animal Falls

*July, 1841. Fleshy material falls from a red cloud over Lebanon, Tennessee.

*August 17, 1841. Flesh falls from a red cloud over Spring Creek, Tennessee.

*February 15, 1850. A red cloud dumps fleshlike substance over Simpson County, North Carolina.

*(month unknown), 1850. Several hundred pounds of flesh is cleared up after it falls from a red cloud over Cloverlea, Virginia.

*December 28, 1857. Lizards shower down over Montreal, Quebec.

*June 11, 1864. Lumps of ice containing tiny green frogs fall over Pontiac, Ontario.

*June, 1869. Flesh and blood rain down on Santa Clara County, California.

*August 3, 1869. A fall of flesh and fine hair is reported in Los Nietos, California.

*(month unknown), 1870. In Sulfur Springs, Texas, a bloody substance rains down.

*August, 1870. Sacramento, California is hit by a shower of lizards.

*March 3, 1876. Thin strips of flesh fall over Columbus, Georgia.

*October 12, 1888. Snails and oyster shells fall during a rainstorm over Brownsville, Texas.

*February 4, 1892. Brown worms rain down over Clifton, Indiana.

*July, 1896. Birds fall dead out of the sky over Baton Rouge, Louisiana.

*June, 1911. Hundreds of salamanders fall over Boring, Oregon, during a rain shower.

*August, 1961. In Capitola, California, birds of all kinds fall from the sky.

*September 7, 1971. Hundreds of fish, each about two inches long, fall on Port Richey, Florida.

Taken as a whole, the hot spots for fall phenomena are the coastal ranges of California, the Portland area of Oregon, Los Angeles, San Francisco, Northern Ohio, and New England. The spot reporting the most fall phenomena is the coastal area just north of Los Angeles.

Dr. Persinger took his analysis of animal falls one step further and quantified the different species as percentages. Rains of fish came out tops at 29 percent, followed by frogs and toads (25%), worms and larvae (12%), insects (11%), birds (6%), lizards and salamanders (3%), spiders (2%), snails (2%), eels and snakes (2%), turtles (1%), clams (1%), crabs (1%), and multiples and others (5%).

So, wherever you go, especially around Santa Barbara or Bakersfield, California, it may pay to take an umbrella along, just in case—except, that is, if you're in Salinas, Kansas, where nothing is likely to protect you from that eighty-pound chunk of ice hurtling out of the sky!

Ghost Lights

The eerie phenomenon of ghost lights is peculiar for more than one reason. Ghost lights are the only member of the transient phenomena family that in some instances may not be true transients. The reason for this is that there are some well known ghost lights—for example, the Brown Mountain Lights in North Carolina and the Hornet Spook Light in the south midwest—that appear, disappear, and reappear at various times.

But the fact still remains that they are mysteries and will remain so until somebody can come up with a single bright reason as to why they should exist at all.

Ghost lights are normally seen from a distance (although not exclusively), usually appear to be quite small (about basketball-size), and may dart around. From many authenticated reports, an interesting factor to emerge is that ghost lights either extinguish altogether, or move away when an observer tries to approach them to find the source. The latter may be a trick of depth perception, as lights in the distance at night could be anything from yards to miles away, depending on their intensity, and this may not be apparent to the observer.

An associated phenomenon is that they are sometimes accompanied by hissing or crackling sounds, an observation that tends to make one think of a natural, gaseous phenomenon that has spontaneously (or otherwise) ignited.

Eighteen verified sightings of ghost light spots have been recorded in the United States.

From the Persinger files:

*In the Chinati Mountains of Texas, ghost lights have been recorded for centuries by native American Indians. They associate them with the souls of the dead.

*Joplin, Missouri. Ghost lights observed since 1901.

*Warrenburgh, New York. Bouncing ghost lights first observed in 1946.

*Suffolk County, Virginia. Ghost lights have appeared since 1951.

*The year of 1951 was also the first time ghost lights made their appearance in Gonzales, Louisiana.

*During a thirteen-year period from 1956, ghost lights were reported from Loudonville, Ohio.

*Fifty years of spook lights have been recorded at Vernon, Alabama.

*The year 1956 was the first sighting of the spook lights of Silver Cliff, Colorado.

Unidentified Flying/Landing Objects

UFOs are the Big Daddies of Fortean phenomena. Since it is UFOs that first come to mind in any discussion of unexplainable events, they need little if any explanation as to the substance of the experience. It would be impractical to catalog every UFO sighting ever recorded, as there are tens of thousands. For his analysis, Dr. Persinger collated a cross-section of 534 sightings, of which twenty cases were clearly based on conversations or meetings with humanoid inhabitants of the craft; the so-called Close Encounter of the Third Kind, a phrase coined by the dean of UFOlogy and a close personal friend, the late Dr. J. Allen Hynek.

Hot spots for UFO encounters are the Los Angeles and San Francisco Bay areas (most probably because of the high population densities), New Hampshire and northern Ohio.

*April 5, 1800. In Baton Rouge, Louisiana, a luminous object believed to be an airship was sighted.

*April, 1897. Reports came from many central states of a cigar-shaped object cruising the skies. Luminous search-light shapes were seen on the craft (the Aurora, Texas, case was among these sightings).

*(month unknown), 1922. A funnel-shaped light descends over Wellstown, Ohio, and is observed for thirty minutes.

*August 17, 1947. Flying saucers circle a lake in Crow River, Ontario, and are photographed by observers.

*September 3, 1947. Saucer seen over Lake Tahoe, California.

*July 14, 1952. Two pilots over Norfolk, Virginia, report bright disks in the sky.

*(month unknown), 1955. A bright orange object lands in Picket Line, Quebec.

*November 6, 1957. A UFO is spotted in a field by a group of young boys.

*April 24, 1964. UFO lands in Socorro, New Mexico.

*August 30, 1964. A cigar-shaped flying object is spotted over Bennett, Iowa. Observers report two lights on its midsection.

*September 4, 1964. A red ball lands in Glassboro, New Jersey.

*February 28, 1970. A saucer-shaped craft is spotted near Culberston, Nebraska, and later tracked on radar.

*August 24, 1972. A football-shaped object lands in Norton Sound, Alabama.

*November 18, 1973. In Rosebud, Texas, a "flying triangle" is reported to have chased two women.

Humanoids

Because so many types of phenomena, both natural and technological, can account for UFO false-alarms, some researchers say the only positive proof of a UFO is when it develops into a so-called Close Encounter of the Third Kind . . . when a creature is clearly visible and connected with the craft.

Whether they are little green men or not, most observers

of UFOnauts describe them as humanoid in appearance, with large, bulbous heads, no apparent ears or noses, scrawny bodies, and sometimes clawlike hands and feet.

*(month unknown), 1954. Three creatures thirteen inches high are seen emerging from a craft in Garson, Ontario.

*November 6, 1954. Claims are made for contact with UFOnauts in Brownsville, Texas.

*November 5, 1958. Midgets are spotted in the area of Pioneer, Ohio, after a strange craft is seen to land.

*April 18, 1961. Occupants of a UFO are reported to have talked to a man and given him food.

*September 19, 1961. Two residents of Franconia Notch, New Hampshire, Barney and Betty Hill, claim to have been taken forcibly aboard a UFO where they were medically examined by alien beings. Hypnotism reveals identical stories.

*November 3, 1971. Humanoids are seen with a craft in Austin, Texas.

*October 11, 1973. Two local residents of Pascagoula, Mississippi, are taken aboard a strange craft where they talk with aliens. Both men later pass lie detector tests.

Strange Areas

These are spots where unexplained events are reported to take place on a regular basis, or areas that are known to exert some bizarre force or affect. Twenty-seven strange areas have been identified.

*Moncton, New Brunswick. Magnetic hill.
*Lebanon, Missouri. A healing stream.
*Santa Cruz, California. Strange magnetic anomalies.
*Chatham County, North Carolina. Nothing grows in a forty-foot diameter spot.

  *Salinas, California. Bizarre gravity effects restricted to a 100-foot diameter spot.

  *Odd Acres, Missouri. Magnetic and gravity anomalies.

  *Barrie, Ontario. Mysterious force pulls cars off road.

  *Scotty's Castle, California. Rocks move within a small area.

Unusual Forces

The following cases are mostly associated with what we term as poltergeist phenomena, and usually relate to a particular home or revolve around one single person. One-hundred-and-forty cases of poltergeist phenomena or unusual kinetics in houses were analyzed.

  *(month unknown), 1790. In Wizzard's Clip, West Virginia, objects are reported moving of their own accord. Animals keel over dead for no reason or disappear from one spot only to reappear in another.

  *(numerous months), 1820. In Tennessee, residents called it the "Bell Witch" period. Objects move, ghostly voices are heard, and sudden unexplained deaths are associated with the phenomena.

  *October, 1873. In Menomonie, Wisconsin, ladies's dresses are ripped to shreds while their wearers are still in them. Objects seen to move.

  *August, 1883. A fifteen-year-old girl causes a stir in Cedarville, Georgia. Objects and pebbles move in her presence. Unexplained rapping noises also heard, and dishes are smashed.

  *January, 1888. Large stones fall inside closed room.

  *September, 1889. In Clarendon, Quebec, fires start spontaneously, rocks move, and people experience their hair being pulled by unseen forces.

  *March, 1892. In Chicago, Illinois, objects move, jewels are smashed, curtains ripped in a home. The actions take place around a thirteen-year-old girl who is sick.

*March, 1929. Buckshot continues to fall for days from the ceiling of a garage.

*(numerous months), 1940. A statue of St. Anne weeps in a Syracuse, New York, church.

*(month unknown), 1952. In San Bernardino, California, a bracelet of unknown metals appears and disappears.

*October, 1953. Water keeps appearing in a house in Orlando, Florida.

*September, 1955. Water collects on furniture in a house in Windsor, Vermont, at the rate of thirteen pails each day.

*February, 1958. Objects move, bottle caps pop off in Seaford, Long Island.

*March, 1960. Portrait of Virgin Mary cries in Hempstead, New York.

*June, 1961. Blood spots keep appearing at a house in Houston, Texas.

*December, 1962. In Toledo, Ohio, objects are seen to disappear and reappear.

*January, 1963. In Edmonton, Alberta, objects and blankets move, and pounding sounds are heard.

*October, 1963. Water sprays out of walls at home in Lawrence, Massachusetts.

*May, 1970. In Oakland, California, rings from fingers and clocks disappear.

*(month unknown), 1972. In a home in Detroit, Michigan, drawers are moved, holes are punched in walls, and knocking sounds are heard.

*July, 1972. Statue of the Virgin Mary weeps in New Orleans, Louisiana.

Spontaneous Fires and Human Combustion

Spontaneous human combustion, a baffling phenomena known as SHC for short, has been recorded for centuries. Charles Dickens even described a vivid example of it in his classic *Bleak House*. Early scientists probing the phenomena attributed it to overindulgence in alcoholic substances —until it was shown that even when human tissue is soaked for days in pure alcohol, not only will it not spontaneously ignite, it will not even continue to burn for more than a few seconds. And that's not even enough to make the rarest of steaks.

Victims of SHC are usually totally immolated in a fire so intense, it reduces flesh to a sticky soot and bones to ashes in seconds. Clothing worn by the victims is most often found to not bear scorch marks. Thirty-one verifiable cases have been recorded in the United States.

*August, 1887. Forty fires hit a single house in a space of weeks. A small child is found in flames.

*May 12, 1890. Female found dead and burnt to a crisp in Ayer, Massachusetts. Her clothing was untouched by the fire.

*September, 1952. In New Orleans, Louisiana, man spontaneously bursts into flames and burns to death.

*March 28, 1953. In Silver Springs, Maryland, an eleven-year-old girl watches, horrified, when her accordian bursts into flames as she plays it.

*May 18, 1957. Sixty-eight-year-old female bursts into flames in Philadelphia, Pennsylvania.

*August, 1958. A house in Talladega, Alabama, is struck by mystery flames. They appear near ceilings and are reddish-blue in color.

*(date unknown). Bed in a home in Columbia, South Carolina, spontaneously erupts in flames.

*October, 1964. Woman aged seventy-five found burned to a cinder in her car. Dallas, Texas, police report that the vehicle was untouched by the fire.

*January, 1968. A house in Ballinger, Texas, is the site of a spontaneous human combustion. The home is reported to have a history of SHC.

Mysterious Etchings and Shadows

Often associated with religious overtones, unexplainable etchings and, in some cases shadows, may be explained by the almost photographic reaction of certain materials after they've been struck by an extremely intense, bright (electrical) discharge, such as lightning. Forty-nine U.S. cases were used in Dr. Persinger's studies.

*(month unknown), 1865. In Demonsville, Kentucky, a rainbow is etched on a window after a lightning storm.

*(month unknown), 1887. A woman's face is etched on a window pane after a lightning storm.

*(month unknown), 1887. During a lightning storm in Hillsdale County, Michigan, the image of a nearby cat was found etched on the head of a bald man.

*June, 1927. Image of Christ appears etched on a window in Belen, New Mexico.

*December, 1957. In Wilmington, Delaware, a family discovers the image of Christ etched on a door.

*June, 1969. Image of Christ appears on a screen door of a home in Port Neches, Texas.

*September, 1971. Shining crosses are found etched on numerous windows in four Florida cities.

*October, 1971. Churches across the state of Georgia report crosses etched on windows.

*May, 1972. Various figures appear on windows throughout Cedar Hill, Texas.

Wild Men and Bigfoots

While there have been thousands of reports of Bigfoot sightings, the following will give an idea of the similarities in description.

*March, 1851. A gigantic wild man is seen in Green County, Arkansas. Indian legends abound in this area.

*July 3, 1884. Primatelike creature captured near Yale, British Columbia.

*(month unknown), 1924. Many observers report a seven-foot, 400-pound, manlike monster.

*September 12, 1952. Ten-foot tall, foul-smelling creature encountered in Flatwoods, West Virginia.

*(month unknown), 1956. Large primate creature spotted in Wadesboro, North Carolina. Believed to weigh about 650 pounds.

*February, 1962. Bigfoot sighting at Fort Bragg, California.

*February 26, 1971. Gorillalike beast spotted in Lawton, Oklahoma.

*July, 1972. Residents of Cairo, Illinois, report a ten-foot-tall monster.

*August, 1973. Over fifty encounters reported of "smelly" nine-foot-tall humanoids.

Unknown Flying Creatures

Birds we know, from the hummingbird to the eagle. But when birds are reported as large as some small houses, that's bound to raise eyebrows. Flying men with giant wings? Well, that's another matter. Twenty-six reports of unidentified flying creatures have been recorded.

*July 28, 1880. Man seen flying with wings over Madisonville, Kentucky.

*(month unknown), 1927. Gigantic bird with a head shaped like a torpedo is seen at Sausalito, California.

*(month unknown), 1948. Enormous birdlike creature seen flying over Santa Barbara, California. Head is shaped like a giant torpedo.

*April, 1948. Scores of people in the towns of Alton, Freeport, and Caledonia, Illinois, report seeing monster birds.

*May, 1961. Giant bird, prehistoric-looking, approaches an aircraft over the Hudson River in New York.

*November, 1966. Numerous reports from Point Pleasant, West Virginia, of a large, winged man.

Sea and Lake Monsters

The world's best known lake serpent is Scotland's Loch Ness Monster. But the United States has its fair share of unexplained lake and sea life. "Champs" is the pet name for the Lake Champlain Monster; Okanagan Lake in British Columbia has "Ogopogo"; "Hapyxelor" lurks in Muskrat Lake, Ontario; "Manipogo" in Lake Manitoba; and, not to be outdone, Lake Waterton in Montana has monsters called "Oogle-Boogles." Clearly the names are picturesque, even if the monsters themselves may not be. Seventeen such monster sites have been recorded in the U.S. and Canada.

*August 19, 1880. A boat on Deschene Lake, Ontario, is reported colliding with a large sea serpent. Later hairlike substances are found in the water.

*October, 1896. Gigantic sea monster found washed up on the shore at St. Augustine, Florida.

*November, 1947. Sea serpent appears before numerous witnesses.

*(various months), 1955. Eight-foot-long sea creature seen in a lake at Bainbridge, Ohio. Historical reports had preceded this sighting.

*August 19, 1963. Forty-foot sea monster reported off the coast of New Jersey.

*April 15, 1969. Echogram detects the outline of a 200-foot-long, four-legged creature swimming in the depths off Kodiak, Alaska.

Impossible Fossils

Fossils have been the subject of many great hoaxes. Two of the best known are the Cardiff Giant, said to be the petrified body of a giant which was later displayed by P.T. Barnum and eventually admitted to as a hoax, and the carefully prepared blending of an aged ape and human skull which fooled science for years and was known as the Piltdown Man.

But some fossils, or objects found in stratas of rock where they shouldn't be, defy explanation. Eighty-one unusual archaeological finds have been cataloged.

*1833. Human skeleton twelve feet long is discovered in Lompock Ranch, California. It is said to have had a double set of teeth.

*1883. Ten gigantic human skeletons found in Warren, Minnestoa.

*1851. Nail found inside a block of quartz in Springfield, Massachusetts.

*1869. Two-inch screw found inside feldspar discovered in Treasure City, Nevada.

*1891. Gold chain found embedded in a coal face at Morrisonville, Illinois.

*1891. Mummylike sarcophagus found in Crittendon, Arizona. Said to have been measured for a man twelve feet tall.

*1968. Fossilized sandal print estimated to be 240 million years old found in Delta, Utah.

In the following examples, the exact years of discovery are unrecorded:

*Baxter Springs, Kansas. Human footprints measuring forty-four by twenty-one inches found in sandstone.

*Western Missouri. Huge human bones found, including a lower jaw.

*Potato Creek, Indiana. Nine-foot-tall skeleton found, with finely worked copper ornaments discovered near the grave site.

*Utica, New York. Skeletons of giants found, all with double sets of teeth.

*Sayre, Pennsylvania. Human skeleton more than seven-feet long found. Estimated to have been buried around 1200 AD.

CHAPTER 5

Raining Cats and Dogs

Of all the fall phenomena, that of animals tantalizes the imagination and boggles the mind. The expression "It's raining cats and dogs!" conjures up just the right illusion for many. But, as we will see, it might be far more appropriate to use the phrase, "My gosh! It's raining fish and toads out there!"

You may find it interesting to note that nobody has actually ever recorded a fall of cats and dogs from the sky—but there have been numerous reports of fish and frogs raining down.

Many theories have been advanced on how these creatures get up in the air in the first place, and most of them, like the hapless animals involved, are hard to swallow. Even those that appear initially quite sound tend to fall apart when the evidence is examined a mite closer and all the factors are taken into account.

It's nice to surmise that a waterspout, a whirlwind, or a tornado, whipped the creatures up into the heavens and then deposited them to a fate of human ridicule. For human ridicule is most often what observers of this phenomena receive when they report such a happening. But as more folk report showers of animals, we have to accept that phenomena like this do exist as a genuine, albeit Fortean experience.

But back to the waterspout theory. In the majority of cases it really doesn't hold water, so to speak, when you try to apply some careful considerations. Yes, it's entirely feasible that a shoal of surface-basking fish could be caught up in a waterspout—but how do you explain it when the sky plungers are deep sea varieties that make their homes in the gloom? How come no seawater falls with them? How do you explain it when they arrive frozen, or "baked" rock hard, or, as sometimes happens, badly mutilated? What's the explanation when only one single species falls in great numbers—to the exclusion of not one fish of another variety?

Then there are the witnesses. When they amount to almost an entire town, there're problems attempting to discredit a whole population of folk. And consider this, which you will read more about shortly: What do you say to a man who not only sees fish falling from the sky, but feels them hitting him, can sweep them up into a bucket, and then take them home for the dinner table? Hardly a figment of the imagination!

Waterspouts, whirlwinds, and tornadoes are children of a Mother Nature on the rampage. Falling fishes and frogs are freaks of nature that don't necessarily have to be connected to her other brats. Why should we expect her to correspond to our human laws of logic?

The Evidence Is Fishy

The following highly credible report, first published in *Science* in 1949, is rather unique. It was made by naturalist A.D. Bajkov who just happened to be visiting the town of Marksville on a field expedition when fish began to rain from the sky.

October 23, 1947. Marksville, Louisiana. "A rainfall of fish occurred on October 23, 1947, in Marksville, Louisiana, while I was conducting biological investigations for the Department of Wildlife and Fisheries. In the morning of that day, between seven and eight o'clock, fish ranging from two to nine inches in length fell on the streets and in yards, mystifying the citizens of that southern town.

"I was in the restaurant with my wife, having breakfast, when the waitress informed us that fish were falling from the sky. We went immediately to collect some of the fish. The people in town were excited. The director of the Marksville Bank, J.M. Barham, said he had discovered upon arising from bed that fish had fallen by the hundreds in his yard, and in the adjacent yards of Mrs. J.W. Joffrion, the cashier at the same bank.

"J.E. Gremillion and two merchants, E.A. Blanchard and J.M. Brouillette, were struck by falling fish as they walked toward their places of business at about 7:45 A.M. There were spots on Main Street, in the vicinity of the bank (a half block from the restaurant) averaging one fish per square yard. Automobiles and trucks were running over them. Fish also fell on the roofs of houses. The several species that fell were native to local waters. They were cold when picked up; one person claimed they were frozen. The fish fell in a strip seventy-five to eighty feet wide and about 1,000 feet long. The weather was foggy but comparatively calm.

"The following species were categorized as belonging to: large-mouth black bass (Micropeterus salmoides), goggle-eye (Chaenobryttut coronarius), two species of sunfish (Lempomis), several species of minnows, and hickory shad (Pomolobus medicris). The latter species were the most common. I personally collected from Main Street and several yards on Monroe Street a large jar of perfect specimens, and preserved them in formalin in order to distribute them among various museums. A local citizen who was struck by the fish confirmed that the fish were frozen. There is at least one record, in 1896 at Essen, Germany, of frozen fish falling from the sky. The largest fish in my collection was a large-mouth black bass, nine and a quarter inches long. The largest falling fish on record was reported from India and weighed over six pounds."

Bajkov went on to report that all the fish that fell at Marksville were perfectly fresh and fit for human consumption. The New Orleans weather bureau had no report of any large tornado or updrift in the Marksville area, and Bajkov estimated that the wind speed at the time was not more than eight miles per hour. "Fish rains have nearly always been described as being accompanied by violent thunderstorms and heavy rain," he pointed out. "This, however, was not the case in Marksville."

Other cases include:

*1875. Woodbury, New Jersey. Small fish found flapping about in puddles after a heavy rain.

*1886. Aberdeen, South Dakota. Small fish found on the roofs of office building after hard rain.

*1888. Little Rock, Arkansas. Fish found in ponds that were dry before a heavy rain.

*Summer, 1890. Grape Creek, Illinois. Small sunfish and many frogs covered a field after a heavy rain. The fish were believed to be perch, and the frogs were three-quarters to one inch long.

*May 29, 1892. Coalburg, Alabama. So many eels fell in a shower that farmers came with carts to take them away for use as fertilizer.

*1893. Winter Park, Florida. Sunfish two to four inches long fell with rain.

*May 15, 1900. Providence, Rhode Island. During a severe thunderstorm, perch and bullpouts two to four inches long fell on yards and streets.

*Summer, 1900. Buffalo, New York. Street puddles filled with small fish.

*June 27, 1901. Tillers Ferry, South Carolina. Hundreds of little catfish, perch, trout, etc., fell during a heavy rain and were found swimming in pools between cotton rows.

*May 18, 1928. Tarboro, North Carolina. Hundreds of small fish were found swimming in puddles in the fields after a heavy downpour.

*July 5, 1825. Kingwood, New Jersey. A four-inch sunfish, still alive, discovered during a violent rainstorm.

Falls of Frogs and Toads

In 1917 a gentleman by the name of Joseph Fairhill, Jr. wrote to a science magazine and related a strange experience he had one summer years before. The event, he explained, took place in 1890 after a heavy rainstorm on a very hot day. And Mr. Fairhill's observation was to raise interesting questions that nobody has yet been able to answer to any degree of satisfaction.

He recalled, "I was in the midst of this walking across a bare tract of land of about 160 acres, which was at least a mile from the nearest water; and I noticed as soon as the rain was over that the ground all around me for some distance was literally covered with small sunfish about one and a half inches long and small frogs at three-quarters to one inch long and that these were as full of life as if they had just come out of the water."

A *Sourcebook Project* researcher William Corliss asks, "How could a whirlwind or waterspout pluck these two different species and nothing else from a body of water, especially when sunfish and frogs do not usually mingle in nature?" An intriguing question, indeed.

Although there have been few or no recordings of frog falls in recent times, the 1800s had a fair share.

*1804. Windham, Connecticut. Frogs shower down over the town.

*1864. Pontiac, Michigan. A small green frog is found inside a hailstone.

*July, 1873. Kansas City, Missouri. A shower of frogs darkened the air and covered the ground for a long distance.

*June 16, 1882. Dubuque, Iowa. Small still-living frogs found in hailstones.

Insect Falls
(from newspaper reports of the day)

*1897. Hutchinson, Minnesota. A luminous cloud "rose majestically from the eastern horizon, shown with a uniform, vivid whitish light and passed directly over the town. When the cloud was overhead a great shower of insects descended to earth, covering the ground all around to the number of about 50 to 100 square feet. These insects proved to be a species of hemiptera and were nonluminous. They had apparently been induced to take wing by the bright object in the sky."

*October 14, 1934. Rock Creek, British Columbia. "It rained beetles at Rock Creek, B.C., Oct. 14. The downpour of tiny brown insects lasted intermittently for three hours. The beetles had wings, but seemed unable to use them.

Bird Falls

While we accept that the most obvious place for a bird to
be found is up in the air, what sets the following reports of
these winged creatures apart is the fact that for some unknown reason their natural habitat in the sky became alien
and horrible.

For birds to depart from the skies, sometimes in suicidal
drives, is indeed unusual.

*1896. Baton Rouge, Louisiana. Contemporary report:
"On Friday morning last early risers in the little capital
witnessed a peculiar sight in the shape of a shower of birds
that fell from a clear sky, literally cluttering the streets of
the city. There were wild ducks, catbirds, woodpeckers,
and many birds of strange plumage, some of them resembling canaries, but all dead, falling in heaps along the thor-
oughfares. The singular phenomenon attracted many
spectators and caused much comment. In the neighbour-
hood of National Avenue, children collected 200 birds."

*March 20, 1941. Shreveport, Louisiana. Newspaper
account: "Blackbirds by the hundreds dropped dead from
the sky at Barksdale Field. They cluttered the army airbase
so thickly that its police were sent out to clear the ground.
A soldier said large flocks of birds broke flight and suddenly plopped to the ground."

*March 13–14, 1904. Minnesota. Report: "Rober tells
the fate of migrating Lapland Longspurs on the night of
March 13–14, which was 'very dark but not cold, and a
heavy, wet snow was falling but little wind was stirring.'
Migrating Longspurs came from the Iowa prairies in a vast
horde, and from 11 P.M. until morning, incredible numbers

met their deaths in and about villages by flying against buildings, electric light poles and wires, and by dashing themselves forcibly into the frozen ground and ice. In Worthington, Minnesota, an attempt was made to compute the numbers laying dead on two lakes with an aggregate area of about two square miles. 'A conservative estimate showed that there were at least 750,000 dead Longspurs there on the two lakes alone!' The total area in which dead migrants were found covered approximately 1,500 square miles."

*December 13, 1928. Caliente, Nevada. News account: "During an early morning hour (about 2 A.M.) of December 13, 1928, residents of Caliente were awakened by a heavy thumping of something falling on the roofs of their houses. Those who were curious enough to step outside and investigate the unusual occurrence found scores of water birds in the new fallen snow. The next morning, several thousand Eared Grebes were found on the ground and on the roofs of business houses throughout the city . . . literally thousands of these birds were found in every portion of the town and on the outskirts . . . they were forced out of the air by the heavy density of snow . . . Caliente had the main bunch, but they were scattered for twenty miles each way." Hundreds more were discovered in various spots in Utah on the same date.

*October 7–8, 1954. Warner Robins Air Force Base, Georgia. News account: "On the night of October 7–8, the largest recorded ceilometer kill in history occurred at Warner Robins Air Force Base, a few miles south of Macon, Georgia. It involved fifty-three species and an estimated 50,000 birds, 2,552 of which of them were examined. An advancing cold front in the autumn is believed to have precipitated these mass mortalities by bringing together adverse weather conditions (especially a lowered cloud ceiling), nocturnal migrants, ceilometers and/or tall obstructions."

*January 25, 1969. St. Mary's City, Maryland. Wire Service account: "Something smashed up flocks of ducks flying over Maryland so that their dead and dying bodies rained down around the southern Maryland community of St. Mary's City (about fifty miles SE of Washington D.C.). Canvasbacks, redheads and scaups were found scattered around St. Mary's River and even in the downtown business section. The ducks had sustained widespread hemorrhages and multiple fractures."

*November, 1973. Stuttgart, Arkansas. News account: "On the day after Thanksgiving, hefty, mature mallards came crashing out of the sky. Many of them were frozen stiff. The day the ducks came tumbling down was a wild and turbulent one in Arkansas. Several twisters were sighted over the state and several touched down amid violent springlike thunderstorms, wind flurries and hailstorms. 'It was about 4 P.M.,' said Lloyd McColum, chairman of the State Game & Fish Commission. 'Within ten to fifteen minutes all of them had come down, all mature, fairly heavy ducks.' The ducks came down with a lot of hail and several were completely ice encrusted, according to witnesses. Possibly they may have been pitched up higher than normal and frozen along with the hail. 'They go up there in a colder atmosphere and, just like an airplane, got iced over,' Mr. McColum said. 'They got ice on their wings and couldn't fly. In short they just froze to death.'"

Miscellaneous Falls of Living Animals

The following are newspaper accounts or details from scientific journals:

*June 18, 1881. Salem, Iowa. "On the night of June 8 there was a heavy rainfall, and on the morning of the 9th, the ground was covered in places with something that looked like blood. I found that they were living creatures, and with a spoon took up a pint of muddy water containing them. Upon examining the sample received, I found it to be swarming with Cyclops quadricornis (a small crablike creature), or what I take to be that species. The only thing peculiar about them is that the body is full of bright red corpuscles, which accounts for them imparting a red appearance to the water containing them. While it might not be considered remarkable that a few of these animals should be found in pools of rainwater, I am puzzled how they came here in such immense numbers, unless we suppose that they were distributed through the whole body of the rain that fell, and were afterwards concentrated by the draining away of surplus water. There was not less than five hundred in the sample of water, of which about one third were alive."

*June 6, 1869. Chester, Pennsylvania. "Mr. John Ford exhibited to the Conchological Section, Academy of Natural Sciences, Philadelphia, specimens of Gemma gemma, remarkable as having fallen, accompanied by rain, in a storm which occurred at Chester on the afternoon of June 6. The specimens were perfect, but very minute, measuring one-eighth inch in length by three-sixteenths of an inch in breadth. Though most of the specimens which fell were broken, yet many perfect ones were collected in various places, sheltered from the heavy rain which followed their descent. A witness of the storm, Mr. Y.S. Walter, editor of the *Delaware County Republican,* assured that he noticed the singular character of the storm at its very commencement, and, to use his own words, 'it seemed like a storm within a storm.' A very fine rain fell rapidly, veiled by the shells, which fell slower and with a whirling motion. Judging from the remains of the animal matter attached to some of the specimens, together with the fresh appearance of the epidermis, it is highly probable that many of them were living at the moment of transition. This minute species resembles a quahaug shell, and is common on the seashore between tide marks."

*It was January 15, 1877 when Memphis, Tennessee, was showered with evil black snakes. An eyewitness account recalls, "Morning opened with light rain; 10:20 A.M. it began to pour down in torrents, lasting fifteen minutes. The wind was SW. Immediately after, reptiles were discovered crawling on the sidewalks, in the road, gutters and yards at Vance Street, between Lauderdale and Goslee Streets—approximately two blocks. Careful inquiry was made to ascertain if anyone had seen them descend, but without success. Neither were they to be found in the cisterns, on roofs or any elevations above the ground. Vance Street is comparatively new, has no pavements, and the gutters are merely trenches. When first seen the snakes were very dark brown, almost black. In some places they lay very thick, entangled together like a mass of thread or yarn."

Although the Great Memphis Snake Fall might most appropriately be assumed to be the sudden emergence of thirsty snakes after a heavy downpour, a report in *Scientific American* concluded that the reptiles had actually been carried up into a hurricane and deposited in Memphis—although this author has not been able to find records of a hurricane having hit in that vicinity during that period of time.

*December, 1857. Montreal, Quebec. A shower of very much alive lizards fell upon the sidewalks and streets.

*July 3, 1860. South Granville, New York. During a very heavy rainstorm, an observer heard something splash into a puddle near his feet. He found a stunned snake and reported that it fell during the storm.

*1873, Minnesota. A shower of unidentified reptiles was reported.

*January 20, 1894. Nashville, Tennessee. During unusually heavy rain, seven young men sheltering under an awning heard a splash and saw a living creature on the pavement. They captured a full-grown salamander (Amblystoma xiphias) ten-and-three-quarter inches long.

*May 11, 1894. Bovina, Mississippi. Person found a gopher turtle, six by eight-inches long that was completely encased in ice. It was believed to have fallen during a heavy hailstorm.

CHAPTER 6

Monsters From the Deep

Farmer Bramblett Bateman was standing on the bank of the White River when something extraordinary caught his eye. It was a Saturday afternoon in July, 1937, the weather was clear, and the time was 1:00 P.M. Bateman moved nearer to the river to get a better look.

What Bateman had seen first was a disturbance in the water. It began to bubble and foam, and then slowly a large object started to break the surface. The farmer hadn't a clue what was going on, but the more he studied the eerie sight from the depths, the more he became convinced he was observing a live animal or giant fish.

By his own account, Bateman estimated the visible part of the creature to be at least twelve feet long and some four or five feet in width. He could see no recognizable head or tail. In fact, the best description might have been remarkably similar to witnessing a whale as the arch of its back breaks the surface. But this was in Arkansas, hundreds of miles inland from the nearest sea shore, outside the town of Newport, on a river that forms a main tributary of the mighty Mississippi.

Fascinated with his bizarre find, Bateman continued to spy on the animal as it basked in the summer sun. The distance between Bateman and the animal made it difficult to form an accurate assessment of color and texture, but the farmer believes the creature had gray, leathery skin. Of one thing he was certain; this was no floating log, upturned boat, or industrial artifact that might have been washed downstream. This was very much a live, albeit unusual, animal.

It continued to wallow on the surface in the same position for about another five minutes when, without any appreciable movement, it slowly sank down into the gray waters of the river and was gone.

This wasn't to be the last time the farmer would encounter the creature that would come to be known as the White River Monster. The next time he would be carrying a rifle and have a police escort in tow.

Monsters Everywhere

A number of stretches of water throughout the United States and Canada can lay claim to having their own monsters. Most of them are inland lakes or large rivers. Some have become tourist traps or havens for monster hunters. Lake Champlain, the massive body of water between New York State and Vermont which runs up to the Canadian border, has "Champs"; Lake Onondaga in upstate New York boasts the "Mosqueto"; Okanagan Lake in British Columbia has "Ogopogo"; the Muskrat Lake in Ontario is the home of "Hapyxelor"; Lake Manitoba has "Manipogo"; Lake Utopia in New Brunswick is proud of its own monster, and Lake Waterton in Montana has a family of monsters with the catchy name of "Oogle-Boogles."

In total, seventeen freshwater sites have been recorded as home for aquatic or semi-aquatic unidentifiable creatures in the U.S. and Canada.

While the Big Daddy of lake monsters worldwide is usually thought of as "Nessie" in Scotland's Loch Ness, reports of monster sightings in American waters date back to pre-Colonial times. Native American Indians recorded sightings of lake monsters for centuries prior to the colonization of the U.S. What's fascinating is that the reports of American lake monsters and their descriptions often correspond exactly to descriptions of the creature that is purported to live in Loch Ness.

Further proof of this is the remarkable similarity between a black-and-white photograph of Nessie, known as the "surgeon's photo" (it was snapped by a noted physician who was visiting Loch Ness) taken in the 1930s, and a color picture snapped in 1977 on the shore of Lake Champlain by Sandra Mansi, a thirty-four-year-old artist and amateur photographer. Each photograph shows a creature breaking the surface. Both have long serpentlike necks and horse-shaped heads and a clearly visible hump or back that appears to be attached to the neck structure. In each photograph there is striking sameness in the posture and the arch of the head and neck.

Over the years, the negative of the famous Loch Ness shot has been examined by photographic experts, including scientists at Kodak, and each time it has been verified as being untampered with and genuine. Mansi's shot has also been subjected to critical review by photographic experts and given the stamp of authenticity.

It's interesting to note that the first recorded sighting of a lake monster in contemporary history was made by none other than explorer Samuel de Champlain, the man who gave his name to Lake Champlain. His observation took place in July 1609, not long after he had been warned by the Indian population that the vast body of water was inhabited by an animal known as "Chaousarou." Champlain was so taken aback by his encounter with the monster that he made a detailed log of it in his diary. The journal entry reports that the creature was some twenty feet long with a neck "as thick as a barrel" and a head that reminded the great explorer of a horse. The legend we know today as

"Champs" was duly recorded into history as the first verifiable lake monster in what was to become the United States of America.

Native American Indian Legends

One of the earliest reports of an aquatic monster comes from the Cherokee Indian nation. The creature, which inhabited the Valley River in North Carolina, was named Tlanusiya—or, roughly translated, "the place of the Leech."

Legend has it that The Leech was first spotted by a group of Indian braves as they followed a trail that ran beside the Valley River. As they rounded a bend they almost stumbled upon it. In clear view, resting on a ledge of rock that spanned the river to form a natural bridge, was a large red-colored creature. The men were puzzled; never had they seen an animal like it. Crouching down in the undergrowth, they began to observe the beast. Then, as the story goes, the huge creature proceeded to stretch out to its full length, like a giant snake uncurling itself.

The Cherokees could clearly see that the monster had red and white stripes along its body. Its length, combined with a slimy appearance, reminded them of a giant leech. The creature rolled itself up once more, stretched again, and then slithered off the rock and into the river. As it entered, the water began to foam and boil, and a huge plume of spray shot into the air.

The legend continues that at this point, the men turned and began to run for their lives, thinking that the monster had spotted them and was making for shore. As they looked back, they saw the jet of water come down in exactly the spot where they had been hiding a couple of seconds earlier. The water-gun effect, they were sure, would have washed them off their feet and into the river—obviously the monster's dastardly way of capturing its prey.

The incident was reported back to the tribe with the warning that crossing the river at that point should be avoided at all costs, lest they fall victim to the monster and its deadly spray. Those who ignored the warning apparently paid dearly since bodies were known to be found mutilated on the banks of the Valley River with their ears and noses eaten off.

According to another legend there was one fearless tribesman who took it on himself to slay the monster. He donned warpaint and his finest buckskins and headed for the river, followed at a safe distance by a curious party of observers from the village. He perched himself atop the rocky outcrop at the river's edge and cried out for the monster to appear and do battle. Suddenly the river began to boil around the rock, a great wave rose up and swept him into the foam. He was never to be seen again.

Other instances of the monster appearing are recorded in Cherokee legend. According to John Parris writing in the Ashville *Citizen-Times*, just before the Great Removal of the Cherokees to Oklahoma in 1835, two fearless Indian women, apparently sick to death of eating "fat meat" were determined to have fish for dinner and went out to fish from the rock ledge. One of the women had been carrying a baby on her back, and as she laid the child down on the rock to prepare her fishing line, the rock was hit by a sudden surge of water. Grabbing her child in the nick of time, the Indian woman and her accomplice dashed for shore before the Great Leech could strike.

While not all Indian legends are quite as colorful or romantic as that of the Great Leech, the appearance of weird or potentially dangerous lake life was certainly first taken seriously by the original natives of North America. Oneida Indian history reports that a great reptilelike monster called "Mosqueto" inhabits Lake Onondaga near Syracuse, New York. Knowledge of the monster goes back centuries. On the banks of Lake Ontario there was supposed to exist a monster so fearful and repugnant that it could knock unfortunate observers over by its terrible stench alone. According to legend, hundreds of Indians had perished in this peculiar way.

Indians inhabiting the banks of Lake Koshkoning in Wisconsin swear to the existence of a large aquatic animal that would constantly play havoc by wrecking their fishing nets. And a farmer living beside the lake claimed that the same monster was responsible for slaughtering and partly eating a number of his pigs that were foraging by the lake.

Early settlers around Alkali Lake, near Hay Springs, Nebraska, were warned by local Indians that a fearful monster lived in the lake. Although no historical accounts of the monster exist today, a relatively contemporary account from July, 1923 sheds new light on the Indian legend.

According to a report in the *Omaha World-Herald*, a duck hunter by the name of J.A. Johnson said he had run into the monster while accompanied by two friends. Johnson also offered that he knew of dozens of other eyewitnesses who had seen the creature over the years.

The three hunters were wading through some reeds just after dawn when they stumbled upon a giant creature laying half-in, half-out of the water. Johnson said he could have likened it to a giant alligator, but the beast was much heavier, thicker and at least forty feet long. He recalled that it had a full tail and a stubby head with what appeared to be a large proboscis or horn between the eyes and mouth. The creature was a dark gray in color.

Johnson and his colleagues stopped in their tracks about twenty yards from the creature, but, having spotted them, it plunged into the waters of the lake and was gone. Johnson was quoted as noticing an unusual aspect to this already strange occurrence. "There was a very distinctive and unpleasant odor noticeable for several moments after the beast had vanished into the water. We stood for several minutes after the animal had gone, hardly knowing what to do or say," said Johnson.

Then there was a foaming and bubbling in the lake about two hundred yards from where the dumbstruck men were standing. "Sure enough the animal came to the surface, floated there for a moment, and then lashed the water with its tail. Suddenly he dived and that was the last we saw of him," Johnson added.

The White River Monster

After Bramblett Bateman's encounter with the White River Monster he blustered into the office of local sheriff Zack Reid, demanding he be supplied with a weapon to enable him to kill the creature. In a signed affidavit, Sheriff Reid recalled, "He asked if we had a high-powered rifle and explained that he wanted to kill a monster he had seen in White River."

Intrigued by Bateman's convincing story, Reid broke out a rifle and rounded up deputy Joe McCartney and civilian Henry Harper. The three men returned with Bateman to the site at about four o'clock. When nothing unusual had stirred after two hours, the men were about to get into their car and head back for town when "A little negro said that something was coming up," remembered Reid. The sheriff went on, "We ran back to the bank and there was a lot of foam and bubbles coming up in a circle about 30 feet in diameter, some 300 feet from where we were standing. It did not come up there but eventually appeared about 300 feet further upstream. It looked like a large sturgeon or catfish. It went down in about two minutes."

Reid revealed that deputy McCartney had attempted to shoot at the creature, but found he'd forgotten to load his gun. "There is no doubt in my mind that it was something alive, but I do not know what it was. We waited another hour, but it did not appear again," added Reid. The sheriff was so convinced of the importance of his experience that he didn't hesitate to give permission for his affidavit to be published.

Thus began a spate of reports of sightings along the White River that would span four decades.

Among the dozens of sightings along with Bramblett Bateman's during 1937, some themes are consistent and have remained so during future encounters with the White River Monster. The beast is almost always described as gray, sometimes with peeling or crusted skin. A head or tail is not always visible, but the monster nearly always appears in a flurry of bubbling or foaming water. The beast also is known to be quite vocal, with most people agreeing that it sounds very similar to the trumpeting of an elephant or giant sea lion.

The White River sightings were taken so seriously that by 1973 citizens collected hundreds of signatures on a petition to the Newport City Board of Directors. It called for the board to approve an official "White River Monster Refuge and Sanctuary" on a portion of the White River next to Jacksonport State Park. The move was so popular that by the end of the year it was sanctioned by the Arkansas Senate, and laws were actually drawn up to protect the creature. It was declared illegal to "kill, molest, trample" or harm the White River Monster in any way while he is in the area of the sanctuary.

After the 1937 sightings, the next major monster flap at White River happened in 1971.

Ernest Denks of Newport first saw the monster in early June. He described the creature in no uncertain terms as an animal and not a fish, at least twenty to thirty feet in length, and weighing upwards of 1,000 pounds. He also noticed a pointed bone or horn on the forehead, another consistent theme among White River sightings.

Later, tracks suspected as having been made by the monster were discovered at Towhead Island. As news spread, it became obvious that others had seen similar tracks in the past, but nobody had thought enough about them to put two and two together and come up with a monster. More sets of tracks were found on the island. One set clearly showed that an animal had come out of and returned to the water. This same set of tracks, however, provided an additional significant insight: in this one area, small trees had been pulled down and a large portion of the undergrowth had been flattened leading one to surmise that some huge creature had been resting or sleeping there.

Sheriff Ralph Henderson of Jackson County ordered plaster casts to be made of the prints which were fourteen inches long by eight inches wide, and displayed three toes on each. The toes also displayed what appeared to be claws.

Two people who may have had an actual too-close-for-comfort encounter with the monster were Ollie Ritcherson, a trapper, and his sidekick, thirteen-year-old Joe Duprey. The two had decided to explore the area around Towhead Island by boat in the hopes of finding some trace of the monster. Suddenly their rowboat was hoisted clear out of the water as something rose up under them. The incident was brief, possibly no more than two or three seconds, according to Ritcherson, and the boat was set back down into the water without damage or harm to its occupants. Although neither Ritcherson nor young Duprey could attest to having seen the monster firsthand (they were in the bottom of the boat and holding on for dear life at the time), their experience raises an interesting point. If it was the monster that surfaced under their boat, it must have had an extremely large and broad back to have balanced the small rowing boat out of the water without it tipping.

But the cap, by far, to all the White River Monster

sightings came with a series of snapshots, the first ever photographic evidence of the monster.

Toward the end of June, two men, Lloyd Hamilton and his stepson Gary Addington, spotted a twelve to fourteen foot long creature swimming in the White River near Jacksonport. They could only observe its back protruding from the water, but described it as "gray and spiny." Luckily, Gary Addington was carrying a camera, and he began to run off shots of the monster. When news of this reached the *Daily Independent* in Newport, the paper offered to have the pictures developed. With much ado, everybody waited anxiously for the negatives to come back from the darkroom—but they were blank. Whether in the rush to go into print, or simply a careless oversight, the *Independent* had put the color film through a black-and-white processing, with the result that the chemicals completely obliterated any image that might have been on the film. However, all was not lost. Another image of the monster was to turn up.

On Monday, June 30, Cloyce Warren, a worker at the White River Lumber Company, set off on a fishing trip with two buddies. They were boating just south of the White River Bridge near Newport when they noticed a huge disturbance in the water. Warren had a Polaroid Swinger camera with him and managed to get off one shot. This time the *Independent* didn't get a chance to ruin the instant-processing film, and they ran the photo in their edition of June 30 together with a vivid description of the event from Cloyce Warren.

Warren was quoted: "What we first noticed was a giant column of water erupt about 200 feet from the boat. Then this giant form rose to the surface and began moving in the middle of the river away from the boat. It was very long and gray-colored. The creature was on the surface of the water only a few seconds. We had taken a little Polaroid Swinger camera with us to take pictures of the fish we caught. I grabbed the camera and managed to get a picture before it submerged. It appeared to have a spiny backbone that stretched for thirty or more feet. It was hard to make out what the front portion looked like, but it was awful large."

The fisherman's picture, although well in focus, was taken at a distance. However, when the shot is enlarged the opposite bank and trees can be clearly seen, giving unusually good reference points for distance and size. In the forefront in the middle of the lake, a large body has clearly broken the surface. Confirmation of this could be gleaned from the patterns of disturbed water around the object. If an actual creature, it could be calculated at between thirty and fifty feet long, with a sizable portion of body having broken the surface and clearly visible. Trailing off behind, and just breaking the surface, are a series of some twenty small humps or crests, which may have given the "spiny" appearance described by Warren. The photograph is unusual, but it's only fair to point out that a submerged, decaying log, buoyed by gases of decomposition, could suddenly pop to the surface, creating an appreciable amount of disturbance in the water—and have a similar appearance to the object in the photograph. This would not, however, account for the giant plume of water that the fishermen claimed to have witnessed.

Oogle-Boogles and Ogopogo?

Oogle-Boogles! Yes, that's what the folk living around Lake Waterton in Montana call their monsters. They claim that there's a whole family of Oogle-Boogles who range in size from baby versions at two and three feet long to giants up to sixty feet. While nobody has ever come forward with photographic evidence of these creatures, the locals are fiercely protective and loyal to the Oogle-Boogles and are attempting to get their existence recognized and classified as an endangered species.

Just north of Seattle, Washington, and over the Canadian border in British Columbia is Lake Okanagan, home to a creature called Ogopogo. The lake, like many associated with the more famous lake monsters, (Loch Ness and Lake Champlain, for example) is a cold, deep lake with depths in places of almost 1000 feet, but the temperature remains a constant thirty-three to thirty-four degrees so consequently it never freezes over. The monster has apparently been around for centuries, for the original Indian name for it was Naitaka. Ogopogo, a more whimsical name, was dreamed up in the early twenties and has since stuck.

What makes Ogopogo so fascinating is that there have been over two hundred reports of the creature over the past two centuries, and there are a number of rock carvings around the lake that depict the monster. It is fairly certain that the depictions are Indian in origin and quite ancient by the standards of the New World. The carvings, or pictographs, have been engraved into lakeside rocks. They show a creature with a long serpentlike neck, a horselike head, a forked tail, and a series of humps running down the back—bearing a striking similarity to the common seahorse.

The monster has also rated its own book, *Ogopogo*, written by Mary Moon, a longtime historian of the Lake Okanagan phenomenon. In it she records what must be the most convincing contemporary evidence for the existence of some unknown form of giant animal life in the lake.

The incident began at around seven P.M. on July 2, 1949. Leslie Kerry of South Kelowna was just about to take some visiting friends, the Watson family from Montreal, out on his boat when the party spotted what appeared to be an animal in the water close by, only some 100 feet away. What they saw was astonishing. The creature appeared to have a serpentlike body and was lying low in the water, apparently feeding or resting. A forked tail was also visible occasionally as it slapped the surface of the lake. At this time, no head could be seen.

Kerry called to his wife up at the house, and she came out to view the animal through binoculars. Meanwhile, eager to get a closer look, Kerry and Watson and his two children began to row toward the creature. Fearful of scaring the kids, Watson decided they should hold back from getting too close.

Back at the house, Mrs. Kerry, having confirmed the sighting with her own eyes, began to alert the surrounding neighbors by phone. One couple, Dr. Stanley Underhill and his wife Joan, also began to track the creature through binoculars.

From the viewpoint of the boat party, the creature's body appeared to be made up of a series of coils or humps that became visible as it raised and lowered itself in the water. For periods of a few seconds it would sink completely and then surface again.

By now the creature had been visible for some fifteen minutes and Dr. Underhill had been taking careful note of its appearance. He is positive the body was smooth and dark gray or black, and he was also able to observe the coiled shape of the body. He estimated that the coils were on average about seven feet apart and rose no more than a foot out of the water. However, Underhill points out that he believes more than one creature may have been involved, because some of the coils appeared to be too far apart to have belonged to one animal.

The creature began to drift, or swim, out into the deeper water, and then suddenly it dove out of sight—only to reappear again some moments later much further out in the lake and creating a noticeable wake behind it. Some observers believed they saw fish jumping around the monster. Whether fish are the monster's staple diet is open to conjecture, but another sighting of Ogopogo also demonstrated that the creature may come up to search for surface basking fish. More than a dozen people working at a cannery in the small town of Naramata at the south end of Lake Okanagan observed a humped, serpentlike creature about twenty-five feet long crossing the lake and leaving a strong wake behind it. From their vantage point, they could clearly see it was heading for a shoal of fish. The sighting, which lasted for only nine or ten seconds, was brought to a premature close when a motorboat came into view and the creature submerged.

Author Mary Moon reports that Candace McDonald, postmistress in the lakeside town of Peachland, actually stumbled into Ogopogo while out taking an early morning stroll with a friend. As the story goes, Miss McDonald and her companion began following tracks on the sandy beach which led them to an animal that was laid half in and half out of the water. As they approached, the creature slid into the lake and disappeared. Miss McDonald didn't tell the story until near her death, many years later. She was afraid that nobody would take her seriously, and she'd be subjected to ridicule.

That there is a strange unclassified form of animal life in Lake Okanagan seems to be beyond doubt when taking into account the vast number of sightings, encounters that involve a number of witnesses seeing exactly the same thing at the same time, and the high credibility of some witnesses. But what exactly Ogopogo is remains anyone's guess—or does it? We'll look at some fascinating theories on Ogopogo later in this chapter.

Up in Alaska's Illiamana Lake lives a family of creatures that have been monitored by the native Aleut Indians for years. The Indians keep a healthy distance from the animals' known homing grounds because, as legend goes, earlier this century one of their fishing boats was overturned by a creature who then proceeded to gobble up a crewman whole.

Added credence is given to the existence of the creatures by pilots flying over the lake's clear, cold waters. They have reported observing wildlife that sounds remarkably similar to the Aleut descriptions. The creatures have been spotted basking on the lake or swimming just below the surface. Local fishermen have reported with some frequency that nets become entangled and completely shredded by an unknown creature of great weight that has always escaped before anyone has managed to haul one to the surface.

According to the Aleuts, the monsters come in a variety of sizes, have long, tapered bodies, possess tails, have broad, squat heads and are a sleek silver in color.

Champs

There's an age-old question that's constantly posed about Champs, the monster said to inhabit the vast reaches of Lake Champlain: Where does he go in the winter?

It's a good point, and one that raises a number of theories. While it's nice to see Champs on a sunny spring or summer day, where does he go when the landlocked lake is completely frozen over with ice that can be many feet thick in the winter months?

There are many imponderables surrounding Champs. However, he's more than just a bona fide legend—he's also a celebrity. Thousands have flocked to Lake Champlain in the hopes of getting a glimpse of the elusive beast, and a handful have not gone away disappointed. There have been some twenty-seven contemporary sightings of Champs that have been accepted as verification that some form of unclassified aquatic animal lives in the great lake.

Sightings of Champs were common as far back as the

late 1800s. Even the greatest showman on earth, Phineas Taylor Barnum, was absolutely enamored with tales of the giant monster. Not satisfied with bringing the world's biggest land mammal—Jumbo the elephant from the London Zoo—to American audiences, he desperately wanted the biggest lake monster. P.T. Barnum believed that Champs could be caught and put on display in his traveling exhibit. As an inducement, he offered $50,000 for the creature he described as the "Champlain Sea Serpent"—dead or alive!

Champlain is the United States' largest body of inland water, next to the Great Lakes, with a surface area of 438 square miles. It has New York State as its left bank, and Vermont for its right while stretching up into the province of Quebec for a total length of 110 miles. In certain areas of the lake, depths can reach over 400 feet. That's quite an area Champs has to make his home—and reports of sightings span the entire length of the lake.

As early as 1819, newsheets were publishing reports of the monster. The *Plattsburgh Republican* ran an article describing how a group of pioneering folk were scared witless when they encountered Champs in Bulwagga Bay near Port Henry, New York, one of the narrower stretches of the lake. Although the report said they only witnessed the monster's head breaking the surface for a few seconds, it was enough to ignite a period of monster madness.

In August, 1878, the yacht *Rob Roy* was at anchor off Button Bay Island with a small party of vacationers on board. Suddenly a monstrous head appeared out of the water. They gazed in awe as the creature swam by, its giant shape clearly visible under the crystal clear, calm water.

A trio of university students spotted the monster in November 1879, this time much further north near Burlington's Apple Tree Point. A good fifteen feet of the monster and its neck were reported to be visible as it sped up the lake in a northerly direction.

And on August 4, 1892, the annual picnic of the American Canoes Association was thrown into disarray as the monster appeared once more. Not known to be weak-kneed souls who'd be perturbed at the sight of large fish, the canoeists however went into a panic as Champs appeared offshore between a whole armada of carefree canoes. The outing was immediately disbanded.

But the crowning glory to all Champs sightings came in recent times when Sandra Mansi, thirty-four, an amateur photographer and artist, captured Champs on film quite by chance. Her photograph has been hailed as the most impressive piece of evidence for the documentation of Champ's existence. Joseph Zarynski, founder and driving force behind the Lake Champlain Phenomena Investigation group, calls the photograph "very impressive—the single most crucial piece of evidence for the existence of Champs."

Mansi's adventure was to prove to be an odyssey of sorts. And her snapshot would become famous after being reprinted in both *Time* magazine and the *New York Times*.

On July 5, 1977, Mansi was sight-seeing in the area of St. Albans, Vermont, one of the widest points on the lake, separated only by Grand Isle from the New York side. She and her husband and two children decided to cut down to the shore to enjoy the view and let the kids paddle.

As the children splashed under the bright sun, Mansi thought she noticed a log or a swimmer break the surface directly out from where the children were paddling. She looked, looked again, squinted her eyes, and tried to rationalize the image.

Then the object didn't seem to fit any of her initial perceptions as it rose higher in the water. Quickly it dawned on her that she was watching a creature, an animal that had a long brown or gray neck with a large, pointed head. She also noticed that the animal was of some considerable size and bulk, with a giant hump or fleshy back. Mesmerized, she stared out past the children at the creature that was positioned between herself and Grand Isle.

She describes it as having slimy looking skin like that of an eel. But this creature was much larger than any eel she could possibly imagine.

Gathering her wits, Mansi yelled to her husband and then dashed back to their car to dig out her Kodak Instamatic camera. She loosed off just one shot of the monster before she and her spouse swept up the two children and headed for the car. The photo was to become a classic. When they turned to look for the monster again, it had disappeared.

It has to be pointed out that Mansi is a rather shy, timid young woman and didn't breathe a word of the picture for more than three years. Eventually, piqued by the serious publicity being gained by the Lake Champlain Phenomena Investigation, Mansi says, she agreed to hand it over to Joseph Zarynski for analysis.

The snapshot (for that's all it was by now, Mansi having lost the original negative) was to be examined by veteran Loch Ness researcher and scientist Dr. Roy Mackal, a zoologist from the University of Chicago, and Dr. Roy Frieden, a professor of optical sciences at the University of Arizona. Frieden found no evidence that the photograph had been tampered with and both scientists agreed that whatever was shown in the snapshot strongly suggested the existence of an unknown, possibly animal or fish form, moving in the lake.

The photograph itself *is* remarkable. A few branches and leaves in the bottom corners of the shot give an important foreground perspective while the banks of Grand Isle and its foliage can clearly be seen across the lake. Some seventy-five yards or so from the Vermont shore is the ominous, looming shape of a gray-skinned creature. Its neck is fully extended, and the head appears to be looking sideways or back over its giant body, which can be seen rising some three or four feet out of water. Mansi claims that the creature she saw was bending its head and neck one way and then the other, as if scanning the lake and shoreline.

What makes Mansi's photograph and story so believable is that the woman may have never gone public with her picture had she not been gently pressured by investigators. In fact, after gaining somewhat of a celebrity status herself among the Lake's devout monster hunters, she related the following at a seminar organized by the Lake Champlain Phenomena Investigation in 1981: "Later my husband and myself had great trouble rationalizing it, so we decided to refer to it as a 2,000-pound duck. It was easier to live with a 2,000-pound duck than something you don't know."

Clearly Mansi had dwelled over the photograph many times and considered that it may have had some significance to science. It is also quite obvious that the image of the afternoon of July 5, 1977 still haunted her. While researching his book *Mysterious America,* author and investigator Loren Coleman was able to gain Mansi's confidence. She told him, "I still have nightmares about the monster. The thing is chasing me, and I'm running to get away. After I saw the monster and took his picture, I had the dreams all the time, but then I got in touch with Zarynski and the nightmares went away for a while. Now with all the public pressure and people saying I didn't really see it, the dreams have started again. It's frightening, and sometimes I wish I hadn't told anyone about the picture—or hadn't seen the monster."

As the legend of Champs grows, Mansi may find that her odyssey is yet far from over!

In 1982, the states of New York and Vermont passed joint resolutions outlawing any harassment of Champs. The laws declared that the creature was protected from any willful act that resulted in its injury.

CHAPTER 7

Was It a Monster?

The theories for lake monsters abound. A lot of them are plain wacky. But there are credible scientists who have earnestly tried to come up with solutions for the monster phenomena.

Roy Mackal is one of these hard-nosed investigators. He's also a very serious scientist. The University of Chicago biochemist and zoologist is famed for his intrepid pursuit of the Loch Ness Monster. He spent fifteen years investigating Nessie and pioneered searches that included sophisticated underwater photography techniques, and scanning the loch with sonar. Dr. Mackal has also turned his extensive talents to analyzing evidence of lake monsters both in the U.S. and Canada.

His theories offer the best solutions cryptozoology may ever have for our monsters from the deep.

Solution at White River?

Mackal has very little doubt about his conclusions for the White River Monster, and this theory may well pertain to other so-called river monsters in the U.S. and Canada. Mackal believes that the monster was merely a known aquatic creature observed outside of its normal habitat.

After analyzing all the detailed descriptions of the White River Monster from the people it was terrorizing around Newport, Arkansas, Mackal is certain the beast was nothing more unusual than a wayward large male elephant seal that probably strayed from its normal waters along the Mexican or Southern California coasts.

It is quite possible for the marine animal to take to and survive in freshwater. Mackal points to a species of ringed seal that has adapted to the freshwaters of Lake Baikal in Siberia where it now makes its home.

The male elephants are the largest of all seals, can weigh in at over 8,000 pounds, and grow to a length of twenty-two feet. Their gray skin color fits well with the descriptions of the White River Monster, and the skin molts each year between May and July (remember, the White River incidents were mostly during June and July). This could give the appearance of peeling skin reported by some observers in Newport.

But what about reports of the monster sporting a horn? A similarity that can't be ignored is that the male elephant seal has an inflatable nose or trunk that can actually droop down as far as the mouth.

The king of seals also is a vegetarian and known to wander as much as forty miles inland, foraging for food. No problem here then, when accounting for flattened shrubs, small trees, and large patches of undergrowth.

Quite simply, the theory is that a large male elephant seal wandered into the mouth of the Mississippi and made its way up into the White River, one of the great river's largest tributaries. To look at it lightly, finding Newport an ideal spot, the giant mammal decided to spend a summer vacation there!

With lake monsters, however, the story is far more intriguing.

Prehistoric Monsters

When it comes to roots, Champs and Ogopogo may be close relatives.

We'll start with the interesting parallels Dr. Mackal is able to draw between Scotland's Loch Ness and Lake Okanagan. Both are deep, freshwater lakes, are well oxygenated and, according to Mackal, have a population of fish "adequate to support a small colony of fish predators, maintained ultimately by connections through rivers to the sea." This connection, or "windows" to the seas, is crucial in Mackal's theories for what the monsters may indeed really be.

In his book *Searching for Hidden Animals,* Mackal makes the following statement: "I hope to lead the reader to the conclusion that there is a serious side to this nonsense and that there is in reality a small population of aquatic fish-eating animals residing in Lake Okanagan and perhaps a few other Canadian lakes."

From voluminous zoological evidence, the scientist is convinced that the majority of so-called lake monsters are in fact, throwbacks to prehistory—prehistoric monsters, in effect, that have by some strange twist of nature survived through the ages. Although Mackal admits we only have the fossil records of these creatures to go by, they make a good model for what people are describing in Loch Ness, Lake Okanagan, and Lake Champlain.

Other scientists have offered the plesiosaur as an answer. The long-necked, extinct marine reptile that propelled itself through the depths with giant paddles instead of fins or feet and arms fits ideally with the sightings described at Champlain and Loch Ness. Of course, there is the question of how they got there in the first place.

The plesiosaur was a reptile that swam in the great prehistoric seas before the continents were formed into the shapes we recognize today. As mountains wrenched upwards under the huge pressures of the changing face of the earth and vast oceans were squeezed into smaller seas and sometimes lakes, it is entirely feasible to assume that some of the wildlife may have been trapped and forced to adapt to a new environment. Plesiosaur could have been a prehistoric species that survived until today in the massive lakes of the American continent.

But what about the lakes that are ice-locked during the winter months? Let's assume that, being a reptile, the plesiosaur was coldblooded. If so then it should be able to live, like a fish, under the thick ice of Lake Champlain. It's also possible that a primitive animal of this type could drift into hibernation during the bitter winter freeze, a state of suspended animation during which its metabolism is so low that it needs neither food nor air as it rests on ledges or at the bottom of a great lake—until awakened in the spring as the water temperatures rise.

A theory such as this may explain why these creatures are able to survive in a landlocked and sometimes frozen lake for centuries without any necessity to seek the sea. It would also help to explain why monsters are never sighted deep into the winter months.

There is also the possibility that there are uncharted access routes to inland lakes, underground tunnels that may interconnect lakes and eventually lead to the sea. It is feasible that Champs could make it through the northern reaches of Lake Champlain and into the Saint Lawrence Seaway—although it would have to navigate a number of locks on the way.

Through an aquatic "subway system" a creature could travel to the oceans before the winters and then return to safe havens, their breeding grounds, in the spring and summer. This, however is pure speculation.

And Dr. Mackal believes it's wrong. His theory is that the monsters, certainly in Lake Okanagan, are actually a small population of very primitive dinosaur-era whales known as *Basilosaurus*. These creatures could easily have adapted themselves from marine to freshwater environments.

Mackal states his case in his excellent and highly readable scientific study, *Searching For Hidden Animals*. "Fresh water could certainly be a suitable environment for a primitive whale, and being warm-blooded it would have no difficulty with the cold water in the depths of Lake Okanagan. Whales are quite at home among the ice flos of the Arctic and Antarctic oceans.

"All whales flex vertically and propel themselves by up-and-down movement of the powerful tail flukes. This characteristic, so well established for the Naitakas (Ogopogos), almost restricts our choice to marine mammals. The single pair of forelimb or paddles of whales are consistent with observations at Lake Okanagan. The top swimming speeds recorded for whales, up to thirty miles per hour in the case of the large finback whale, are remarkable. Many species are easily able to keep pace with modern seagoing vessels. Again, the reported swimming speeds of the Naitakas match the known performance of whales."

The scientist points out that the shape of the Ogopogo head, broad and tapering toward the snout, is exactly what has been found through fossil remains of the skulls of Basilosaurus. He also suggests that the ridges or platelike formations sometimes associated with Ogopogo sightings correspond very well to exoskeletal bony plates found among fossils of prehistoric whales. And with hair or long bristle being common among many types of whales, this could lead to a physical misrepresentation of ears or other appendages.

The descriptions of the monsters of Lake Champlain and

Loch Ness differ from the Canadian lake monsters in so far as both Champs and Nessie are almost always described as having long necks. Mackal admits that at least one underwater photograph and reliable close-up observations all point to long-necked creatures with a thick body (most unlike our image of the whales we see today). This single fact presents a problem in lumping the monsters together as all members of the Basilosaurus family.

But Mackal offers a tantalizing theory.

All whales at one time were land mammals. The Basilosaurus was descended from a line of prehistoric creatures called creodonts, a group of mammals which possessed a variety of neck configurations—including elongated necks. The fossils we can see today of Basilosaurus quite clearly show that their neck vertebrae had not shortened as much as our present day whales have done during the evolutionary process. It would be sensible to theorize that the monsters of Lake Champlain (and Loch Ness) might be an entirely different branch of the Basilosaurus family that were directly descended from the long-necked creodonts!

And Mackal adds another fascinating, thought-provoking twist to the prehistoric whales theory. During his searches of Loch Ness, Mackal and his fellow scientists were able to record "unidentified animate sounds" that came in pulses similar to the echo-locating sounds emitted by whales.

One Last Monster

The wonderful tale of the Great Silver Lake Monster is an episode in history that's well worth recounting. It offers an interesting perspective to close this chapter.

The time was early evening on July 13, 1855. On the shore of Silver Lake in Wyoming County, New York, a group of men and boys were just about to turn in their reels and call it a day. To their horror, looming toward them at a rapid speed across the lake was an incredible-looking monster. Some said it must have measured at least sixty feet in length, others just remembered the piercing red eyes.

The fishermen bolted for higher ground, leaving their catches in buckets and pails for the monster to devour.

Soon there were many more reports of the monster. It was described as a serpent, sixty to one hundred feet long with scaly, dark green skin covered in yellow spots. Most agreed it had flaming red eyes, a huge sharklike mouth with razor-sharp teeth, and giant fins.

It wasn't too long before word spread of the Silver Lake Monster, and folk invaded the little village of Perry in droves to catch sight of the great beast. Perry, at the tip of the lake, became the hot spot for monster expeditions, and the Walker House, a local hotel, became the focal point for intrepid hunters to swap tall tales.

For the next two years, thousands were to pass through the portals of the Walker Hotel. If not having witnessed the monster themselves, they could sit enthralled at the hotel bar, listening to stories of the monster related by the likes of Truman Gillett, a lively local character, or the hotel owner A.B. Walker. The monster was a hit, and so was the Walker Hotel.

But then tragedy struck. On the night of December 19, 1857, the Walker House burned to the ground. And amongst the smoldering debris a sinister discovery was made—the remains of the Silver Lake Monster.

Gillett and Walker were later to confess all. They had built the monster from waterproof canvas, wire, and paint. Using an ingenious flotation device, they were able to pump air into the monster through a hose, and it would periodically rise to the surface. Then it was a simple matter of towing it around the lake by means of a series of submerged ropes.

CHAPTER 8

Devils and Humanoids

Police Officer Sackville will go down in history not so much for his crime busting, but more so for being the first law enforcement officer to encounter the Jersey Devil face to face.

Whatever Sackville's first name was, it has not been preserved for posterity. But on January 17, 1909, in Bristol, New Jersey, Officer Sackville was on foot patrol in the vicinity of Buckley Street. The time was 2:00 A.M. when he first became aware of an inordinate amount of howling and barking among the local canine population. Instinct told him that something, somewhere nearby was not quite right. The diligent cop decided it was his duty to investigate.

Following the trail of noise, he found himself approaching a bridge down by the Delaware River. Something out of the corner of his eye gave him a start. Feeling a little uneasy, he peered down into the gloom over the Delaware and thought he saw an object move again on a towpath slightly below him. The officer stopped and was preparing to illuminate the area with a lantern.

What he saw jump out of the shadows defied all human logic!

A "thing," humanlike with a scrawny body but also large wings, was hopping up and down just a few yards away. Sackville stood rooted to the spot. He had his wits about him enough to slowly reach for his revolver.

As the officer pounced forward with gun drawn, the creature let out an eerie screech and began to hop away. Sackville gave chase, but as he began to close the gap the bizarre apparition before him began to beat its batlike wings. Afraid that the creature would escape, the policeman blasted off a single shot. As he did it swooped up and out over the river. Sackville fired again, but by this time the monster had disappeared into the darkness.

Not too far away, also at around 2:00 A.M. another poor soul was to view a vision from hell. Whether the sighting of the next highly credible witness—this time Bristol's postmaster, E.W. Minster—was before or after Officer Sackville's is open to debate. The interesting point is that they occurred around the same hour.

Minster was having a sleepless night at the time, and decided to bathe his head with cold water, a practice he found to be a surefire cure for insomnia. Minster was so sure of what he saw next out of his bedroom window that he repeated it with gusto (and not the least bit of embarrassment) to reporters the next day. He was quoted in the press as saying:

"As I got up I heard a strange sound coming from the direction of the Delaware. It was an eerie, almost supernatural noise. I looked out upon the river and saw flying diagonally across what appeared to be a large crane, but which was emitting a glow like a firefly."

When Minster was asked to elaborate on his sighting, he gave this incredulous-sounding description: "Its head resembled that of a ram, with curled horns, and its long, thin neck was thrust forward in flight. It had long, thin wings and short legs, the front legs shorter than the hind. Again, its mournful and awful call—a combination of a squawk and a whistle, the beginning being very high and piercing and ending very low and hoarse."

Another shaken witness also came to light. He was John McOwen, a resident of Bath Street, who had experienced something extraordinary at the same early morning hour as well. Rooms at the back of McOwen's home looked out over the Delaware Division Canal. A strange noise had brought him out of a deep sleep and to one of the windows. He peered out into the night to see if he could discover what was causing the ruckus.

McOwen described to reporters what he heard: "It sounded like the scratching of a phonograph before the music begins, and yet it had something of a whistle to it. You know how the factory whistle sounds? Well, it was something like that. I looked from the window and was astonished to see a large creature standing on the banks of the canal. It looked something like an eagle . . . and it hopped along the towpath."

The accounts from the night of January 17 were bizarre, indeed, but they quickly began to take on a certain pronounced credence. Other witnesses of the "Jersey Devil" started coming out of the woodwork, claiming also to have seen a bizarre animal prowling in the depth of the night. And as word spread, the terrified observers popped up not just in Bristol, but in nearby Trenton.

Trenton residents living down by the Delaware were reported to have been so frightened by the screeching and squawking sounds that pierced the freezing night air, they were too scared to venture out of their homes to investigate.

One was E.P. Weedon, a Trenton City Councilman. According to Weedon, some "awful" noise awakened him from a deep sleep. He sat bolt upright in bed when he realized it sounded like somebody was trying to break his door down. He could also hear a flapping of wings.

Councilman Weedon scrambled to a second-floor window. The noise had stopped now, and he peered nervously through the curtains. Below him he saw nothing but the gentle slope of a snow-covered porch roof beneath him. And then it hit him. In the snow on the rooftop he could clearly see prints. But they weren't footprints—they looked like hoofprints.

Another Trenton resident, John Hartman, reported seeing a large, airborne creature with giant wings circle his yard and then fly off into the night. A group of workers at the Hilltown clay bank in Camden were said to have thrown down their shovels and ran for their lives as a giant avion circled high above and then went into a dive toward them.

Even more convincing was the physical evidence the Jersey Devil was said to have left behind. At the Trenton State Arsenal hoofprints—not in fours, but in pairs—were discovered in the snow. And in Bristol, a Mrs. Thomas Holland was reported as having found paired hoofprints in the snow covering her backyard.

In fact, 1909 was the year of the Jersey Devil. Sightings came from towns and cities such as Woodbury, Wycombe, Huffville, Mount Holly, Haddenfield and Manatua. The Devil's path was said to have been a swath cutting through the state some sixteen miles long and three to ten miles wide in places.

Mrs. Leeds You Have a Lovely Daughter

The Jersey Devil certainly caught on. It's been the state's official demon since the 30s, and even today some sports teams are named after it.

But we may have a curious woman called Mrs. Leeds to thank for all this devilishness.

The origin of the legend of the Devil can be traced back almost two centuries earlier, when the goodly Mrs. Leeds of Esteville, New Jersey, gave birth to a monstrosity of a child in 1735. According to the legend, the repeatedly

pregnant woman became exasperated when she discovered
she was with child yet again. After twelve previous little
Leeds kids, it might be said it was unlucky thirteen. Mrs.
Leeds cursed the very thought of having another brat and
vowed that as far as she was concerned, it might as well be
a little devil.

Well, when the blessed event came to pass, Mrs.
Leeds's wishes came true. The child was said to have been
born with cloven hooves instead of feet, a monstrous animal's head, and a bird's body—complete with a large set
of wings. Apparently able to speak at birth, the offspring
promptly let out a tirade of oaths against his poor mom and
flew up the chimney of the Leeds's home, never to be seen
again.

While this may have been quite a relief for the astonished new mother, folklore tells that the "Leeds Devil" was
often spotted flitting through the swamps of the Pine Barrens where it had made its home.

Jersey Devil Captured?

Yes, that's what the newspaper headlines screamed in the
early 1920s.

At last people were going to be able to witness the beast
firsthand, thanks to a certain Norman Jeffries of C.A.
Brandenburgh's Arch Street Museum in Philadelphia, who
was going to put the monster on display for all to see.

Mind you, Mr. Jeffries was not unknown for his tend-
ency to overexaggerate some of his museum's strange and
bizarre exhibits. But sure enough, this time it sounded like
Jeffries had got the real thing because the beast had been
captured live by a bunch of farmers.

The public, however, had been well primed for this
event. Only a few weeks earlier, the Jersey Devil had sur-

faced again after being dormant for years. One farmer's wife, Mrs. J.H. Hopkins, was reported to have run into the beast crouching behind a barn on her land. After the "Devil took off in surprise," Mrs. Hopkins had been able to examine his hoofprints clearly imbedded in the ground.

Now an expert from the Smithsonian Institute also surfaced to say that whatever animal the Jersey Devil may be, he was sure it was a freak throwback to prehistoric times. Somehow a family of pterodactyls had managed to survive and were probably living in the state's remote Pine Barrens. These creatures are known without doubt to have existed—fossilized remains prove that—and they bear an uncanny resemblance to descriptions of the Jersey Devil. Half reptile, half bird, they had an ugly pointed head with a crest, large, weblike wings, and spindly, birdish legs.

Back to the farmers and Mr. Jeffries. The good men of the earth who cornered the beast did, in fact, find something—and with no little persuasion eventually turned it over to Mr. Jeffries who announced it would be displayed at the Arch Street Museum.

Amid great publicity, Jeffries secretly transported the Devil to Philadelphia and then flung open the museum's doors to the hoards of curious visitors who mobbed the building in the hope of seeing the famous spectacle. And disappointed, they were not. The bizarre animal was alive and hopping around its cage with such a "menacing countenance" that visitors were advised not to get too near to the bars.

Jeffries's find was the talk of the times. Alas, it was also a giant hoax.

In 1929 Jeffries confessed he had purchased his monster from a dealer in Buffalo, New York, and planted the bizarre creature in a wooded South Jersey area, where he was sure it wouldn't be too long before somebody stumbled upon it. So what was "it"? Simply a common kangaroo with large, bronze wings attached to its back and stripes painted up and down its body!

Mini Monsters

"It had three legs on it, two little short arms, a short body. It was about four-and-a-half feet tall, and had pink eyes as big as flashlights. I know it wasn't no human being or any type of animal I've ever seen!"

Those were the words of Henry McDaniel of Enfield, Illinois, as he described the bizarre humanoid that he'd just taken pot shots at with a .22 pistol. At the time, the creature was running from his home. The encounter on April 25, 1973, started a monster media blitz in Enfield which was to go on for weeks as reporters and intrepid researchers tried to get to the bottom of the mystery.

The incident actually started with the McDaniel children, Henry and Lil. A few hours later, when McDaniel and his wife returned to their home, they were met with a strange tale from the excited kids. They swore that a small animal-like person had been peering through windows and trying to get into the house. They had heard scratching sounds coming from an outside door, and wrenching sounds from an in-window air conditioning unit.

Not entirely convinced, but intrigued nevertheless, McDaniel picked up his six-shot .22 pistol and a flashlight and went in search of the monster. The time was about 9:00 P.M. "I saw him almost at once," says McDaniel. "He was in the yard and I caught him in the flashlight. But he was startled and took off, running through brush alongside the L&N railroad tracks near the house. He moved like lightning. I'd say he easily covered fifty feet in three jumps." It was then that McDaniel loosed off four shots from the pistol. "I knew I hit him with the first one, because I heard him yelp and hiss like a wildcat," recalls McDaniel.

When news of the creature spread, serious researchers and curiosity mongers alike invaded the small town of only 800 people. The hullabaloo had tempers fraying, especially among the police department, and White County Sheriff, Roy Poshard, Jr., threatened to jail any outsider for disturbing the peace or trespassing while in pursuit of what he firmly believed was a hoax.

A group of monster hunters claimed to have seen what they described as a gray humanoid figure—possibly a monkey—moving through some underbrush. They shot at the thing with a .22 rifle and three shotguns, but it escaped their hail of lead. Twelve days later, a similar creature appeared again—but this time the observers included a more credible witness.

Rick Rainbow, news director of WWKI radio station was with two friends when they spotted what they believed to be the creature late on a Sunday afternoon. The light was fading, but the three men were able to distinguish a humanoid appearance that stood erect but stooped over and was gray in color. They estimated the height of the thing at about five feet. They saw it cowering in the shadows behind an old abandoned house, not too far from where it was originally sighted, at the McDaniels residence. News director Rainbow, who was carrying a portable tape recorder, claimed that he was able to record a scream the animal let out when it spotted the men and took flight.

And in the early hours of the same day, Henry McDaniel claimed once more to have seen the creature. This time it was about 3:00 A.M. and McDaniel said he had been awoken by the howling of neighborhood dogs. Suspecting that the creature might be out there again, he went out along the railroad tracks. This time he was unarmed. Within a few minutes he saw it come out from some brush and begin to walk alongside the tracks. "He wasn't going anywhere fast. He was just ambling on down the tracks and didn't appear to pay any heed to me," says McDaniel.

Strangely, the same area in Illinois was reported to have been plagued by a similar creature some thirty years earlier. According to newspaper accounts in 1941, residents of Mt. Vernon, about forty miles from Enfield, repeatedly encountered a small, humanlike creature that was "like no animal or man" ever seen before.

The sightings started when the Reverend Marsh Harpole reported a weird encounter with a baboonlike being that jumped out of a tree at him. Apparently, the minister was strolling leisurely along Gum Creek when a large animal pounced down and started walking on hind legs toward him. Harpole, who had been intending to hunt squirrels, was carrying a loaded rifle. The startled minister did the first thing that came into his head and took a swing at the creature with the butt of the rifle. Then he fired a couple of warning shots in the air, and the unidentifiable beast took off.

Later that year, hunters in the area reported finding strange, humanlike tracks in the soft mud along the creek bottoms near Mt. Vernon, and soon came reports of howling and screaming noises emanating from the area of the creek at night. A bizarre incident some weeks later was to incense the local populus, mainly farmers. According to press reports, a farm dog had been found dead and horribly mutilated. The conclusion was that such a dastardly act could only be the work of "the creature." A posse of farmers ganged together, loaded to the gills with armaments, munitions, ropes, and nets and set out to corner the beast once and for all. After days of scouring the bottomlands of the creek they returned home empty-handed.

The creature was never to be heard from again.

CHAPTER 9

Bigfoot

Paul Freeman is a big man and tough to boot. Standing at six feet five inches tall and weighing in at over 260 pounds, the U.S. Forest Service Ranger was not the sort of gentleman you'd want to get on the wrong side of: Not the sort of person to shy away from a little bit of trouble if it came his way. Neither is he the type of character you'd expect to have flights of fantasy or sully his professional reputation as an expert woodsman by inventing weird tales.

But on the morning of June 10, 1982, Paul Freeman *did* put his reputation on the line.

Freeman, whose craggy looks, moustache and receding hairline give him an uncanny likeness to screen tough-guy Gene Hackman, was on patrol in the Umatilla National Forest in the Walla Walla district of Washington State. It was a crisp, sun-drenched morning, and the visibility was excellent. This is a part of America that is so wild and untouched that it's about as close as you come to the way God might have originally intended it to be. The rugged mountainous region is a haven for every type of wildlife. Elks and bears are commonplace.

Driving up a steep, unpaved incline, Freeman spotted a group of elks on a distant ridge. He stopped the truck and got out to have a better look to see if the group contained any young, recent additions to the native elk population.

It's a common practice among rangers to try and keep a tally of new offspring for Forest Service records.

But something else caught the thirty-nine-year-old ranger's eye as he trekked up an old logging spur to gain a better vantage point to view the family of elks.

Recalls Freeman, "Suddenly I noticed a figure step off a bank down toward the roadway. As I turned toward it, I thought my eyes were fooling me. My first impression was that I was looking at something that reminded me of all the illustrations I've ever seen of prehistoric man—large, covered in hair, and looking like a cross between a man and an ape."

Freeman, who is a man well accustomed to recording wildlife, knew instantly that this was no bear. "I can spot a bear at a distance of a mile or so across open terrain. You know instantly how their profiles look and their special gait. Even when raised on hind legs, a bear is unmistakable. This was no bear—of that I'm absolutely sure." And by Freeman's estimate the strange figure was less than seventy yards away from him and in full view. The ranger shielded his eyes from the sun to get a better look.

What Freeman saw was an apelike figure, about eight feet tall and covered with reddish-brown hair. The hair was thickest on the shoulders, arms and legs. The skin color that could be seen on the face and upper chest was that of lightly tanned leather. As Freeman stared at the strange beast, it stopped and began to eyeball him back. "It was a weird experience," says Freeman. "He seemed about as curious of me as I was of him. I've been working in the wilderness for years, and I've never seen anything remotely like what I saw that morning. I've never truly believed in Bigfoot stories, but I've never totally discounted them, either. If there is such an animal as Bigfoot, I'm positive that's what I saw."

What gave this sighting so much credibility were some of the cool and well calculated observations that Freeman made in the few seconds he viewed the beast. He knew, for example, that the approximate height of the beast was around eight feet because he could use his experience of estimating the heights of forest animals by comparing them with surrounding trees or vegetation. He also estimated its weight at well over 300 pounds. A crucial observation was that he could hear the beast breathing heavily and could clearly see the chest muscles heaving, as if it had been running. If anyone were to ask Freeman if he thought it could have been a practical joke with somebody dressed up in a gorilla costume, he had an answer for that, too. "The way I saw the chest muscles moving, and the muscles of the arms, legs, and shoulders as he moved, that was something that nobody could duplicate in a suit."

Freeman had taken a few steps closer to the beast, but stopped when he sensed that he might be compromising his safety by scaring the animal into an attack situation. He also admitted he was becoming increasingly nervous when he saw the hair on the neck and shoulders of the beast begin to rise—just as the hair on a dog or a cat rises in an aggressive pose to make their bodies look larger than life to a prospective combatant. Prudently, Freeman began to backtrack. "As soon as he saw me do that, he turned his back on me and ambled off down the road. At that point, I lost sight of him."

But Freeman was also to bring hard evidence back to civilization to confirm his bizarre encounter—plaster casts of the massive footprints the creature had left behind . . .

Popular Sites

Bigfoot reports are nothing new to America. Native American Indians were recording them in drawings, legend, and song long before Columbus set foot on these shores. To them, he was known as Sasquatch. But it wasn't until one incident in 1958 that a lukewarm public began to take Bigfoot reports seriously: This was when a man by the name of Jerry Crew was able to document eighteen-inch long, eight-inch wide humanlike footprints that he'd found on a logging trail in Northern California. Crew said that he found the footprints around his tractor while working in a remote part of the forest. Although at first Crew believed, because of the enormous size, that the tracks had to be made by a bear, they struck him as distinctly odd for bear tracks, which he'd seen many of during his logging years. When wildlife and anthropological experts were to confirm that the toe configuration of the tracks were anything but bear and something similar to human, the world began to sit up and take note. The Bigfoot phenomenon began to hit the minor columns of the daily papers and the front pages of the tabloids. Bigfoot was about to hit the big time.

Although some are more recognized as traditional Bigfoot havens than others, most notably the cold, often wet, and often impenetrable forests of the rugged Northwest, and into the lower reaches of Canada, which harbor more reports than anywhere else in the country, Bigfoot reports come from just about every area of the country. Contrary to popular belief, Bigfoot doesn't confine himself solely to cooler climates. Florida also is a favorite haunt of Bigfoots.

Over 1,000 case studies of Bigfoot sightings in the U.S. and Canada have been recorded by Janet and Colin Bord in a research project they conducted called *Bigfoot Casebook*. The Bords are considered among the foremost experts on the elusive creature. In their book *The Evidence For Bigfoot*, the researchers state that the majority of sightings have been made in British Columbia, Washington State, Oregon, and California. But the beast has been spotted in most all of the American states, from Florida in the southeast with forty-two reports, to Alaska in the far north with ten sightings.

In fact, Bigfoot seems to be just about everywhere. So how come only a small fraction of the population has ever been lucky, or unlucky enough for that matter, to come face-to-face with one? Surely in a country that has 240 million inhabitants, you wouldn't think there'd be many places for creatures the size of Bigfoot to hide. Wrong! As anyone who has flown the length and breadth of the Continental U.S. and seen it from the air will confirm, there are great expanses of wilderness, hundreds of thousands of square miles, that have still yet to be touched by human hand. The populated area of our land mass is but a small fraction compared to the whole.

Characteristics

Bigfoot may take on any number of different guises, just as there are many variations in the ape kingdom. Even among man we see variety, although mainly in facial features, color, and stature only. And that is exactly the same pattern that has been observed among the Bigfoot family of creatures.

Descriptions of the facial features of Bigfoots vary little —a large, wide nose, full lips, big teeth, and a flat face, more often than not with a heavy, protruding forehead ridge immediately above the eyes. Some reports of Bigfoot have noted crests on the creature's head, or the head coming to a conical point at the top rear of the skull. This feature is also seen among certain species of gorillas and orangutans.

Color varies between the beasts; browns, dirty orange, black, and even snow white, being mostly the order of the day. Some Bigfoot spotters have reported the hair being black or gray with white tips, especially around the neck, shoulder, and back areas—very reminiscent of the large male silverback gorilla. The skin color of these creatures has been variously reported as looking heavily tanned and leathery, to negroid black.

Weight and height are two factors that all observers seem to agree on—Bigfoots are giants, and they tip the scales at a far higher level than the average man. Weights for Bigfoots average around the 300 pound mark, but observers have claimed seeing beasts that could easily have weighed in excess of 600 pounds, or about the same weight as a medium-sized bear or a young bull. Most creatures are between the six and seven foot mark, but some reports have stated that they topped ten and even twelve feet.

There are some factors that Bigfoots all have in common: No noticeable neck, the head always appears to start directly at the shoulders; they are all powerfully built, with the good muscle structure you would expect from a serious body-builder, without being fat; they walk predominantly on two legs, unlike the great apes. There are obvious differences between male and females; males sometimes have noticeable genitalia, and females nearly always display large, pendulous breasts.

There is a great variation in the reported eye colors, from glowing red to deep black. The glowing reds are mostly reported by those who've encountered a Bigfoot in the dark, and then the majority of those have been in the glare of headlights or flashlights. An interesting fact to note is that daytime animals' (diurnals) eyes will give a red reflection (remember the "red-eye" effect sometimes captured on those family photos taken with flash?), while pupils of night animals, the nocturnals, will reflect a greenish-yellow hue. As most night sightings of Bigfoot produce "red-eye" reports, it might be safe to assume that members of the Bigfoot family are diurnal, much like humans.

A powerful stench is sometimes associated with sightings of the creatures, but by no means is this the norm. It might be as little as ten percent of encounters that produce a noxious odor. But for those who do feel the full effect of this smell, the experience is memorable. "The odor was overpowering . . : an indescribable stench, really sickening. It almost knocked me over," was the way one person who had a close encounter with a Bigfoot described it. The smell of a Bigfoot has been variously likened to the stench of decaying meat, a septic tank, rotting vegetable matter (especially rotten potatoes), unwashed armpits, or even that of a circus ring once the elephants have arrived.

Footprints

Any law enforcement officer will attest to the value of footprints, no matter how small the fragment of print. In the case of Bigfoot sightings, footprints are an added bonus, and many have been full prints with good depth. The size of the print can give anthropologists and forensic experts an extremely accurate indication of not only height, but also of general bone structure. The depth of print, depending on the medium it was made in, can give a good impression of total weight. Bigfoot footprints have led to some surprising conclusions.

The first thing Ranger Freeman did once he lost sight of his Bigfoot was to drive to the nearest Forest Service cabin and telephone for colleagues to come out with photography equipment and materials to make casts of any available footprints. They were lucky. The creature—or creatures as it turned out—had left twenty-one medium to full tracks. They turned out to be some of the best documentation ever left behind by Bigfoot.

The tracks were identified as belonging to two creatures because of a surprising factor. When they were examined by anthropologist Professor Grover Krantz of Washington State University, the impressions were so good that he was able to detect skin patterns from the casts. These dermal ridges, almost impossible to fake, are much the same as fingerprints from the hands. In this case, they clearly indicated that two beasts had been around at the site of the sighting. Ground conditions at the time were moist, and some indentations sank to an inch in depth. Dr. Krantz was able to estimate the weight of the creatures at around 600 pounds. The prints weren't exactly like human feet because they showed little or no arch in the foot. Bigfoot, it appears, is also Flatfoot. But they clearly showed a human-like big toe followed by four descending toes on each foot. The feet displayed massive proportions, being fourteen inches long and seven inches at the widest part. The stride of the beasts were also enormous—some six to eight feet, compared to the three feet an average man might make.

As Dr. Krantz announced at a press conference held at the University of British Columbia, "The tracks were made by what appears to be a higher primate, but it is neither ape nor human. We have an interesting problem here, because they come from a higher primate that supposedly doesn't exist!"

More Famous Sightings

In March, 1851, in Green County, Arkansas, a "gigantic wild man" was seen. He was described as about eight-feet tall and covered in long, dark hair. Local Indian legends had recorded the presence of a hairy giant in the area for generations.

On July 3 near Yale, British Columbia, a party of trappers announced that they had actually captured a giant ape-like creature resembling a man. No further claims or record of this sighting exist today.

The year was 1924 and in Flagstaff, Arizona, dozens of reports came in that a 400-pound "man-thing" was stalking the surrounding area. On September 12 in Flatwoods, West

Virginia, a ten-foot tall "foul smelling" creature was observed. Four years later in Wadesboro, North Carolina, another outbreak of Bigfoot sightings: This time the creature was estimated to weigh at least 650 pounds. Fort Bragg, California, February, 1962, a "Bigfoot" is sighted which corresponded well with what local native Indian legends had been saying all along. On February 26, 1971, in Lawton, California, residents reported seeing a "gorillalike" creature. A seven-foot tall, "smelly," black-haired creature was seen in Louisiana, Missouri, in July, 1972. In July of the same year a ten-foot tall monster was reported in Cairo, Illinois. And in Westmoreland County, Pennsylvania, in August of 1973, a rash of Bigfoot sightings were recorded that indicated at least fifty different sightings of nine-foot tall "humanoids" that gave off a foul odor.

Bigfoot, it seems, *is* just about everywhere!

Payette National Forest, Idaho, April 7, 1980. One man who should know what he's seeing, and whether it's an animal or not, is Donald Hepworth of the Ontario Humane Society. As a Chief Inspector with the society, Hepworth had handled bears, and even apes, as part of his job. At fifty-four years old, Hepworth had an extremely distinguished background—one that would adequately qualify him as "a trained observer." He is a former member of the London Metropolitan Police Force and was with Canadian Military Intelligence. Hepworth is not a man whose word you would take lightly.

Yet, as he drove on Highway 95 through the Payette National Forest, he had an experience he might have doubted himself. He came across not one Bigfoot, but two!

Hepworth estimated he was as close to them as eight yards when he came to a stop after spotting the pair in the distance in his headlights. One of the creatures was larger than the other, and Hepworth formed the distinct impression that whatever species of animal or primate they were, they were probably juveniles. Although powerfully built, they also seemed immature and almost gangly. The larger of the two beasts he estimated at around five-feet, eight-inches. The other, about two inches smaller. As the larger of the two, who was walking about two or three steps in front of the other, turned around to look at Hepworth, he noticed the obviously protrudent genitalia. Both were covered head to toe with short, black hair, which Hepworth likened to the coat of a short-haired dog.

The former cop and intelligence officer instinctively made mental notes: The creatures appeared to have no necks and extremely broad shoulders. The skull structure was primitive and sloped back from a heavy brow. On the top of their heads were crests of bone or hair. "I recalled the beginning sagital crest of a young gorilla," Hepworth was to state later. What happened next was to confirm in Hepworth's mind that these were certainly no humans dressed up in monkey suits.

To the right of the road was a six-foot high vertical embankment. On the other side was a sheer drop-off to the forest below. The smaller creature stood in front of the embankment and, in one standing jump, leaped to the top and vaulted over. The larger creature followed in two swift bounds. Both disappeared into the darkness. To Hepworth, this ease of scaling a six-foot obstacle was beyond normal human capability. He described it as "an extraordinary display of locomotion." Hepworth added, "I doubt if any human could duplicate it."

Mason County, Kentucky, October, 1980. The Fulton family was sitting around watching TV in their rural home in Mason County when it happened. One of the family heard what sounded like somebody trying the handle to the back door. Charles Fulton went to the door to investigate and when he opened it came face to face with a large creature with long white, shaggy hair.

The "thing," taller than the seven-foot high door post, was standing on the Fulton porch holding a rooster in one hand. Also witnessing the event was Fulton's mother-in-law, standing right behind him in the doorway. The creature looked startled and jumped off the porch. As it stood in the yard and turned back to look toward the house, Fulton aimed his .22 pistol and fired two rounds. Recalls Fulton, "I'm an expert shot. I know I didn't miss—but the creature never flinched." Unperturbed, the creature sloped off into nearby woods at a leisurely pace.

After the story made the local press, Fulton received calls from reporters, he maintains, in over forty states. The price of his going public with his experience: much joshing and ridicule from his neighbors and local townsfolk. But despite the embarrassment, Fulton still says, "I know what I saw. I don't care whether people believe it or not."

Ellington, Connecticut, August, 1982, around midnight. Farmhands John Fuller and David Buckley reported to police that they encountered a Bigfoot sitting on a feed bunker when they went to check on cows at Valley Farms, on Connecticut's Route 83.

As the pair rounded a barn, they stumbled onto the Bigfoot sitting on the bunker, watching the nearby cows. The creature had one hand in the feed as if it was either eating the silage or playing with it. Buckley described it as about six-feet tall, with immense muscles, long, dark-brown hair over its entire body, and arms that hung down to its knees. He estimated the creature to have weighed at least 300 pounds and was able to observe a "good set" of dangerous-looking teeth.

Either sensing the two, or hearing them, the creature jumped up with a start and faced the two terrified farmhands. What happened next, said Buckley, might have been a gesture of friendship—the beast began to walk slowly toward them with his arms outstretched. Fuller, the farm's night manager, screamed, and the Bigfoot turned and fled around the corner of the feed bunkers to vanish into the night. "We had the impression he might have wanted us for dinner," said Buckley later.

In shock, the two men called the Connecticut State Troop Barrack C in nearby Stafford. Although the troopers had a hard time believing the two men, officers were dispatched to search the area. When nothing turned up, the troopers came to an official conclusion: The two farmhands had been the subjects of a hoax by someone wearing a gorilla suit. Commented Buckley, "I can't believe they'd think that. Anyone who'd walk around in a gorilla suit in the middle of the night on farmlands that are likely to be patroled by hands with guns, has either got to be out of their cotton-pickin' mind, severely brain-damaged, or straight suicidal!"

An Eerie Tale

The Indians have never doubted the existence of Bigfoot. To them, we may seem very naive in our disbelief. In fact, some tribal legends claim that their folk were even on friendly terms with the creatures. Take the example of a Wintu medicine woman by the name of Flora Jones.

Bigfoot researcher Tom Muzila was fortunate enough to be able to pick the brains of Flora Jones when she agreed to be interviewed by him in 1978 at her home in Lake Shasta, California. Her story is provocative.

As Jones tells it, the Wintu tribe has long considered Bigfoots as a giant primitive race of Indians. She revealed that it was common knowledge that the Bigfoots were a hardy race that matured very slowly and lived to a great age. She said that they were different from humans in that they did not produce many offspring, and then only at long intervals. She was positive the race was on the decline, and for that reason, she explained, there were presently only a handful of Bigfoots left in the Lake Shasta area.

According to her recollections, the creatures lived in caves, and it wasn't uncommon for her people to find uninhabited Bigfoot dwellings which were easily identifiable because of the extremely large human-like bones that could be found scattered on the cave floors. The tale gets wilder.

Jones explained that the Wintu people were the only northern California tribe to ever be able to continue a long-term relationship with the Bigfoots. The relationship was so cozy that the Wintus would even trade tobacco with their giant friends. For what purpose the Bigfoot "tribe" might utilize tobacco, or conversely, whether it was the creatures who were supplying the tobacco, was not elaborated upon.

Whether you take the Bigfoot phenomenon seriously or not, the wealth of evidence for their existence from eminently credible witnesses is hard to ignore. Maybe it is better that they remain with legendary status, because if one is ever captured (alive or dead), it will turn the scientific community upside down.

CHAPTER 10

Miracles and More

When Father Henry Lovett, a Roman Catholic priest and an authority on miracles, heard of a religious statue in Philadelphia shedding blood, he was indeed curious—but mostly skeptical.

That wasn't so, however, among the hundreds of folk of the parish of St. Luke's Episcopal Church in Eddystone, Pennsylvania, who'd flocked to view the statue once it was put on display. The Reverend Chester Olszewski, pastor of St. Luke's, told the press on January 20, 1976, "Hundreds have come to my church to pray before the statue. There's no doubt it has bled. Yet it stands on a shelf ten feet above the altar where nobody can touch it. It has bled as long as four hours. Several times I've seen the palms dry—then minutes later have observed droplets of blood welling out of the wounds. I know there can be no trickery."

The story of the bleeding statue started shortly after Easter of 1975 in the Philadelphia home of Mrs. Anne Poore. The statue, a twenty-eight inch tall effigy of Christ, had been given to Mrs. Poore the previous year and had hitherto shown not the slightest sign of divine intervention. But when the good Mrs. Poore knelt down before it to pray about the way more people were turning their backs on religion, she got the shock of her life.

"Suddenly I looked up at the statue . . . and my heart

stopped beating," she said. "Two ruby-red drops of blood had appeared over the plaster wounds in its palms! Actually, I was terrified. I could see it was real blood."

According to Mrs. Poore, she witnessed more spontaneous blood-letting during the following days, and she invited neighbors in to watch as it was happening. Astounded, friends urged her to hand it over to a church so that others could share in the "miracle," and Mrs. Poore contacted nearby St. Luke's.

Despite the fact that the statue was now firmly lodged in an Episcopal church, Fr. Lovett decided to conduct his own investigation. On arriving at St. Luke's, he removed the hands of the statue (which were attached by simple dowel rods) to ensure that there were no tubes or cavities leading to or in the hands which could give the illusion of bleeding palms. The Catholic priest also observed the bleeding phenomenon for himself firsthand, and was impressed. So much so that when the press got wind of the bizarre story, he announced with confidence, "I think the purpose of this miraculous and unexplainable bleeding is to call our attention to the plight of falling religious values throughout the world."

There's also a nice scientific twist to Mrs. Poore's statue.

Leading Philadelphia physician, Joseph Rovita, M.D., was given samples of the blood and had them tested for composition. His findings were to conclude that not only was the blood from the statue of human origin, but it also was of unidentifiable antiquity. He based this assumption on the numbers of red blood cells found in the samples. Relatively fresh blood contains an abundance of red corpuscles which, with time, decompose at a predictable rate. There were so few red cells in the statue samples that Rovita was unable to identify the blood category and could only conclude that it was "very old."

If the intentions behind the Eddystone bleeding statue

were to call attention to religion, that it certainly did. During the early part of '76 newspapers across the nation gave it wide play. If its intentions were at all ecumenical—to help draw the different religions together—then it was a dismal failure. For there is a sad footnote to this story. Later that year, Fr. Olszewski was given the axe from St. Luke's by his Episcopal elders. The reason? The priest, who had been highly influenced by the statue, had begun celebrating the Roman Catholic Mass in its honor.

Weeping Madonna

Religious artifacts are not only known to bleed, but they can weep with the best of us. And so it was for Mrs. Pagona Catsounis of Island Park, New York, when she found that a framed picture of the Blessed Virgin Mary she had stored away in the attic had suddenly started to shed tears.

Whether these were tears of loneliness after being locked away in the dark for several years, we'll probably never know. But it's enough to know that after that evening in March, 1960 when Mrs. Catsounis first noticed the phenomenon, the lithograph began to draw hundreds of people once the news slipped out. In just one week, over five-thousand people had inundated the Catsounis home, pleading to view the miraculous portrait.

The Reverend George Papadeus, Mr. and Mrs. Catsounis's parish priest from St. Paul's Greek Orthodox Church in nearby Hempstead, was the first man of the cloth to examine the weeping Mary. He reported, "When I first saw it I noticed a tear was drying beneath the left eye. It wasn't long before another tear welled up in the left eye, starting as a small, round globule of moisture in the corner of the eye until it grew and slowly trickled down the Blessed Virgin's face. I was astonished."

With great pomp and ceremony, Fr. Papadeus blessed

the Catsounis home. Photographs were snapped of the picture, and from that point the saga of the weeping Madonna was destined to have no more of a future than to start collecting dust in newspaper archives around the country. It is said to never have wept again.

A Bleeding Christ

The family called it a miracle, a parish priest said it was a "ticklish" situation, and a medical technician confirmed that human blood was being shed.

The mysterious happening which started on May 29, 1979, involved a pocket-sized portrait of Christ in the home of Mrs. Willie Mae Seymore of Santa Monica, California. The small print was encased in plastic and was tucked behind glass in the bottom right hand corner of a picture frame which contained a larger photograph. The first person to spot the picture bleeding was an in-law of Mrs. Seymore's, who noticed what looked like a tear of bloodlike substance begin to form under the right eye of the Christ image.

After a few hours the tear had grown, and now a trail of red ran down the portrait and began to coagulate at the bottom of the picture frame. Not knowing what to make of the situation, Mrs. Seymore called her local parish priest for advice. But the "advice" was abrupt and to the point. "This is a case for the archbishop's office," Mrs. Seymore was told. The local priest refused to view the portrait, and when contacted by the press he would only comment that the occurrence was a "ticklish" situation.

Nevertheless, a local newspaper brought in a medical technician from a nearby hospital to take samples of the substance. After testing, the expert confirmed that it was indeed human blood that was seeping out of the picture. He was quoted as saying, "This is honest-to-gosh, bona fide blood!"

A newsman who was one of the first to inspect the portrait declared that the blood was "still wet" and was flowing directly out of the plastic coating that covered the print. He also attested that there was nothing on the reverse side of the picture, that could account for the strange phenomenon.

Although the picture did not shed any new blood, by week's end, over 200 people had visited the Seymore home to view the "miracle."

Portrait of Tears

An unusual twist on the weeping portrait theme comes from Reverend William Rauscher, rector of the Christ Episcopal Church in Woodbury, New Jersey. Rev. Rauscher, author of *The Spiritual Frontier,* is firmly convinced that he was witness to something akin to a miracle during his early seminary days as a trainee priest.

As Fr. Rauscher tells it, he was in the room of a friend by the name of Bob Lewis who was also attending the seminary. Close to being ordained, Lewis began to reminisce about his grandmother who had wept tears of joy when she discovered that he was going to enter the priesthood. How he so wished she was still alive to witness his ordination.

What happened next still puzzles Rauscher, but he is insistent that without any reasonable explanation for the following event, he believes he witnessed a paranormal event.

No sooner had Lewis said the words about his grandmother than a framed picture of the lady standing on a piece of furniture in the dormitory began to weep.

Rauscher recalled, "Examining the picture, we found

that it was wet inside the glass. The photograph of Bob's grandmother was soaking wet, dripping, with a small pool of water spreading under it. That was genuinely puzzling. The back of the picture, made of dyed imitation velvet, was so wet that the velvet had streaked and faded."

The priest went on to explain that they removed the snapshot from the frame, but the photograph refused to dry for a few days. And when it did, a puffy area was very visible around the face area, as if, says Fr. Rauscher, the tears had originated there and run down from the eyes.

Prophecy of Doom?

Can statues react to nuclear holocausts? Well, according to Allen Demetrius of Pittsburgh, Pennsylvania, they can.

The day was infamous in history—August 6, 1945—when the first atom bomb was dropped on the Japanese city of Hiroshima. Mr. Demetrius was the proud owner of a bronze statuette of a Japanese girl, and on that very same day he noticed tears running down the face of the bronze. Not knowing what to make of the incident, he called on a few neighbors to come over to his home and verify for themselves that the statue was indeed weeping. Nonplussed by the bizarre occurrence, somebody called in the press, and Demetrius recounted the happening and displayed the statue.

The statue was to make news again thirty-four years later. Still in its same spot in the Demetrius home, the bronze unexplainably began to weep again on March 18, 1979—ten days prior to the Three Mile Island nuclear accident in the same state. Demetrius told the press that he believed the statue was trying to deliver an omen of the danger that was to come.

Stigmata

One of the best recorded cases of stigmata in the U.S. involved a ten-year-old black girl by the name of Clorette Robinson of Oakland, California. The story was reported by United Press International and flashed to newspapers around the country on March 24, 1972—although the incident began occurring some seven months earlier.

Clorette was in a classroom at the Sante Fe Elementary School when she first noticed that the palm of her hand was bleeding. The blood was forming in the locations normally accepted as being the site of Christ's hand wounds when he was nailed to the cross.

A teacher was the first to notice the stigmata when Clorette complained that the blood was messing up her school papers. She was quickly dispatched to the school nurse who, after examining the young girl's hand, said she could find no trace of a puncture wound and could not understand why the blood was seeping through her skin.

Dr. Ella Collier, a staff pediatrician at the Kaiser Foundation in Oakland was quoted as saying, "I cleaned away the blood and wrapped her hand in a thick 'boxing glove' dressing. There was no way she could have slipped anything into the bandage or undone it without my noticing. Yet when I unwrapped it some eighteen hours later, the inside of the bandage was soaked with blood. I cleaned the hand once more, and then, as I watched, a drop the size of a small pea began to appear and ran down the palm."

Next to examine Clorette was San Francisco psychiatrist Joseph Lifschultz, M.D. He reported he could find no personality disorders with Clorette. In fact, she was a normal, well-adjusted young girl.

Then the phenomenon was to take a bizarre turn. A few days later, the intensity of the flow suddenly increased—

and this time the blood was running out of both hands, her feet, side, and forehead.

Clorette was immediately rushed to a local hospital where emergency room staff shook their heads in disbelief and admitted they could do nothing to staunch the flow.

At the rate of bleeding, one doctor warned the parents that Clorette might have to undergo a blood transfusion. A short while later, the flow did decrease and Clorette was no longer considered a candidate for emergency treatment.

The blood stopped altogether on March 31, just as suddenly as it had started. No recurrence had been reported.

An interesting note is that the girl's family was protestant, and Clorette attended the New Light Baptist Church in Oakland.

The Exorcist and Poltergeists

While not exactly in the miracle class, exorcisms could be considered as somewhat "supernatural."

If the movie *The Exorcist* had one value to society, it was the fact that the resulting publicity brought out the true facts behind the Georgetown, Washington, D.C., case it was based on. Authorities from the Catholic Church had kept the records hush-hush since it was first investigated by priests in 1949.

The subject was in real-life a thirteen-year-old boy who was only identified by the first name of "Roland." According to official church documentation of the case, the teenager lived with his parents and his grandmother in an upper-middle-class home in Georgetown. The bizarre happenings began occurring on January 15, 1949, when knocking and scratching sounds were first heard in the house.

The noises were followed by instances of small household objects dematerializing and popping up in the most unexpected places around the home. A reading lamp, for example, would disappear from sight only to be found in another room hanging from the ceiling. Not only did these strange happenings surround Roland, but they also followed him to school and erupted in the classroom. The poltergeist phenomena were frightening to say the least, but they did not involve any physical harm to the boy or anybody else.

If Roland's family worried about the psychokinetic happenings, they would have been terrified to hear what was coming next.

Not only did Roland begin to talk in his sleep and yell filthy obscenities into the night—he also began to levitate. Stark horror was how his family described the first of many levitations they would have to endure. Awakened by Roland's screaming, his parents rushed into his bedroom to see him floating, covered by his bedsheets, in midair.

Being not overly religious, but at least true to their faith, the parents sought the help of their Catholic parish priest. It was hard to accept the thought of demonic possession, but the parents had no other explanation. At first they thought it was some manifestation linked with the recent demise of a close relative. Next to be blamed was Roland's aunt who, prior to the poltergeist phenomena, had been teaching the youngster how to use a Ouija board (a number of cases of so-called demonic possession in England were attributed to use, or maybe a better term would be abuse, of Ouija boards).

During the weeks to follow, Catholic priests as well as Roland's parents were to witness the astonishing levitations. Firmly convinced they were dealing with a genuine case of demonic possession, the priests slapped the church's version of a gag order on the whole affair and drafted in specialists to handle it: The exorcists were brought in.

Now things turned from bad to worse. Not only was

Roland flying off around his bedroom at will, he took on a distinct second personality which would utter the foulest oaths and threats at the priests when they were in attendance, and the boy would go into violent seizures. Eventually Roland was committed to a Georgetown hospital for his own safety where the levitations, the devil voices, and the seizures continued unabated.

Unlike the movie version of the event, not just one priest and a noted priest-exorcist were involved. According to official records, the exorcists were Father Raymond Bishop, Fr. F. Bowdern, and Fr. Lawrence Kenny. Realizing that the official rite of exorcism would have to be performed, the priests moved Roland to a Catholic hospital in St. Louis, Missouri.

As well as the exorcists, other priests were brought in to observe the proceeding and take notes. A meticulous diary was kept which detailed the case minute by minute. A typical example of a normal day's proceedings would be a description of how the boy, being held down on his bed by attendants, would develop superhuman strength, cast aside his protectors and literally fly around the room, often rising up to the ceiling and staying there for minutes on end while the priests below were subjected to a tirade of oaths from the voices that came out of the unfortunate boy.

During the attacks of evil, the hospital room would turn ice cold, so much so that the priests would have to muffle up in gloves and overcoats just to enter the room. When Roland was spoken to in Latin, the thirteen-year-old appeared to understand perfectly and would even converse in the language.

And if you are wondering how this case came to be written up as the book, *The Exorcist*, here's the connection.

One of the observing priests was Marquette University's Father Charles O'Hara. Fr. O'Hara was called in from Wisconsin to witness the affair. A good friend of his was

Father Eugene Gallagher, a teacher at Georgetown University—and one of Fr. Gallagher's students was William Peter Blatty, who was eventually to pen the bestseller. It is to be assumed that Blatty somehow gained full access to the facts of the case through Fr. Gallagher, and used them to write an account that was partly fictionalized, obviously to protect the parties involved.

Later probing by the media was to uncover hitherto secret Catholic Church files from the case and bring it to the attention of the public.

Will the Real Exorcist Please Stand Up?

In the Blatty version of *The Exorcist*, the central character is an old, but tough-as-nails, priest who is pictured as the world's foremost expert on exorcism. One immediately gets the impression that the numerous fights the priest has had firsthand with the devil have sadly taken their toll.

Well, the character could possibly have been based on a real-life priest by the name of Father Theophilus Riesinger from Marathon, Wisconsin. Although Fr. Riesinger is not recorded as having being involved with the Georgetown affair, he was to admit later in life, shortly before his death, that he had officiated with the rite of exorcism in no less than twenty-two cases of demonic possession—and he was involved in one exorcism that was as equally bizarre as the case of Roland.

The case first came to light in 1928 in Earling, Iowa, and involved a middle-aged woman who to this day has never been publicly identified. The woman was so bizarrely possessed that she was taken secretly to Milwaukee so that Fr. Riesinger could have complete control over her case.

The woman had first displayed signs of satanic possession as early as her twenty-sixth year—and she was to be the subject of repeated exorcisms. At the time of her first attacks, she lived in Milwaukee, and Fr. Riesinger had performed the first act of exorcism on her. When the woman started to suffer repeated bouts with the devil later in life, Fr. Riesinger was the natural choice. During the months of August, September, and December, 1928, the exorcisms were performed in the rectory of St. Joseph's Church in the presence of parish priest Father Joseph Steiger.

Although the church files on the woman have never been opened to the public, the most graphic (and a presumably authentic) account of the affair was recorded by a priest, Father Carl Vogt, in a small circulation booklet titled *Begone Satan!* Fr. Vogt had interviewed all the witnesses to the case, including Fr. Riesinger. The housekeeper at St. Joseph's rectory, Teresa Wegener, who was witness to much of the goings-on during the exorcisms, signed an affidavit attesting to the authenticity of Fr. Vogt's account in his book.

Fr. Vogt describes how the woman was struck by a series of convulsions during which times disembodied voices would be heard in the rectory and rapping noises came from the walls. During the actual rites of exorcism, the woman was said to have possessed incredible mind-reading powers so that she could completely second guess the actions of Fr. Riesinger and repeat his thoughts and the thoughts of other clergymen who were present.

Unlike the Georgetown affair, only one instance of levitation was witnessed. It happened during the first session of exorcism while church helpers held down the woman as she writhed on a cot and cursed in the foulest of language. Suddenly the attendants were flung aside, and she sailed up to the ceiling. There the possessed woman lodged herself in a corner of the room, glowering down at her tormentors and refusing to budge. It took the combined muscle power of four clerics to finally wrench her from the ceiling.

Because of the official church veil of secrecy, Fr. Rie-singer never discussed it in public, and it has never been documented whether the exorcisms were a success or not.

Miracle Cures

While France has its miraculous Lourdes, and Belgium its miracle of Fatima, the United States has Father Ralph DiOrio, a Catholic priest in Worcester, Massachusetts.

Fr. DiOrio, as well as having his mysterious powers investigated by just about every tabloid, spiritual publication, and parapsychological organ in the country at one time or another, actually made it to television as well. An entire segment spotlighting Fr. DiOrio's cures was run on NBC-TV's *That's Incredible* series in September, 1980.

And the priest is the first to encourage investigation of his healing miracles.

Born in Providence, Rhode Island, in 1930, Fr. DiOrio is an immensely cultivated, educated, and intelligent man who has no fears of himself being exposed through trickery or chicanery. He gained a degree in theology and was ordained a Roman Catholic priest when he was twenty-seven years old. He also has a M.A. in education, a B.A. in psychology, and is fluent in at least half a dozen languages.

It was because of his command of Spanish that the priest was assigned to a Hispanic community in Worcester, Massachusetts. Yet his powers of healing were discovered purely by chance.

Many of his congregation desired a more uplifting form of worship and approached Fr. DiOrio to ask him if he would convert from the staid Catholic services to more of an old-fashioned revivalist, charismatic ritual. A little worried at the thought of instigating this rather radical break from tradition, Fr. DiOrio sought the guidance of his bishop. Surprised when the bishop agreed to his parishioners' requests, the priest flung himself headlong into making the charismatic services a success.

It wasn't long before word spread and people were pouring into the small parish church to experience the soul-soaring chanting and singing of this new style of worship. Probably it was inevitable that the congregation would eventually call for signs from God, especially through healing.

Fr. DiOrio began to practice laying on of hands during ceremonies and encouraged his congregation to pray for healings. Within weeks healings were in fact being reported publicly.

One of the first and most impressive concerned Leo Parras, who had been crippled and wheelchair-bound for years after an industrial accident while still only a teenager. Later surgery to help repair the back injuries only resulted in Mr. Parras leaving the hospital totally paralyzed from the waist down.

His case was considered hopeless, and over a period of twenty years in a wheelchair Mr. Parras's legs became so wasted from atrophy that doctors decided nothing further could be done for him other than to try to ease the constant pain through regular doses of the narcotic-based painkillers Percodan and Demerol. It was a doctor who actually advised Mr. Parras to look into Fr. DiOrio and his healing services.

Mr. Parras was driven by friends from his home in Easthampton, Massachusetts, to Fr. DiOrio's ministry. The priest prayed over Mr. Parras, and, according to all reports, the results were immediate and extremely profound. Mr. Parras arose from his wheelchair on the spot and was able to walk right out of the church. Not only was he walking on legs that were certified by men of medicine to be so atrophied that they would never support his weight again, but Mr. Parras acknowledged that for the first time in over two decades he was perfectly free from pain.

The case of Mr. Parras formed the lead for the *That's Incredible* feature on Fr. DiOrio. Also to be interviewed for the show was Mr. Parras's family physician, Mitchell Tenerowicz, M.D., chief-of-staff at Northampton's Cooley Dickinson Hospital. Dr. Tenerowicz confirmed that he had examined Parras a short time after the healing service and was amazed to see that he could actually walk into his office unaided. The physician admitted that the state of atrophy in his patient's legs had not changed, and he had no medical explanation on how he was capable of standing, let alone walking!

Another remarkable healing performed by Fr. DiOrio was to restore the sight of a little tot who had been born blind in her right eye. She was two years old when Kelly's parents, Mr. and Mrs. David Paquin, took her to see Fr. DiOrio.

The priest was visiting St. Anne's Church, Worcester, not far from the Paquin home in Southbridge. The Paquins didn't really expect to see Fr. DiOrio, but as luck would have it they bumped into the priest as he was strolling around the church grounds.

The Paquins were quick to say that they had brought Kelly to Fr. DiOrio in the hope that he may be able to help restore some of the vision in her blind eye.

Kelly had been born without sight in the eye as a result of a complication suffered by her mother during pregnancy. After she was born, a series of ophthalmologists confirmed that, due to heavy scarring in the eye, there was no possibility it would ever be functional.

As little Kelly stood looking up at the priest, he gently held his hands above her head and began to pray. Her parents were amazed to see her blink, rub the eye, and say that she could see shapes out of it. That part of the healing process had been instantaneous—and it was to dramatically improve during the next few days. When the Paquins took Kelly to have her vision retested by their family physician, he reported that she now had 20/40 vision out of the right eye.

What makes Kelly's case even more miraculous is that, like Fr. DiOrio's healing of Leo Parras, the physical damage was still present, yet for some unfathomable reason a cure had been affected. The physician who examined Kelly said the heavy scar tissue that had previously blocked her vision was still obvious and in place, and he had no explanation for how vision was possible through the previously blind eye.

Today Fr. DiOrio still performs his miracles with the full backing and approval of his bishop and diocese of Worcester. He is director of the Apostolate of Healing and Christian Renewal, and performs healing services on a regular basis at St. John's Church in Worcester.

Bibliography

(* denotes bulletins, journals, newspapers and periodicals with references too numerous to catalog individually)

*American Journal of Science**

*American Meteorological Society Bulletins**

*American Naturalist**

*Annals and Magazine of Natural History**

*Annals of Philosophy**

*Annual Register**

*Arcana of Science**

Bord, Janet and Colin, *The Evidence For Bigfoot*, Aquarian Press, Wellingborough, England, 1984.

*Canadian Naturalist**

Corliss, William R., *Earthquakes, Tides, Unidentified Sounds and Related Phenomena*, The Sourcebook Project, Glen Arm, Maryland, 1983.

Corliss, William R., *Handbook of Unusual Natural Phenomena*, Anchor Press, New York, 1983.

Corliss, William R., *Lightning, Auroras, Nocturnal Lights and Related Luminous Phenomena*, The Sourcebook Project, Glen Arm, Maryland, 1982.

Corliss, William R., *Rare Halos, Mirages, Anomalous Rainbows and Related Electromagnetic Phenomena*, The Sourcebook Project, Glen Arm, Maryland, 1984.

Corliss, William R., *Tornados, Dark Days, Anomalous Precipitation and Related Weather Phenomena*, The Sourcebook Project, Glen Arm, Maryland, 1983.

Coleman, Loren, *Mysterious America*, Faber & Faber, Inc., Winchester, MA, 1983.

*Edinburgh New Philosophical Journal**

*English Mechanic**

Fort, Charles, *The Complete Books of Charles Fort* (*The Book of the Damned, Lo!, Wild Talents, New Lands*), Dover Publications, Inc., New York, 1974.

*Fortean Society Magazine**

*Franklin Institute Journal**

*Globe**

Hunt, Gerry, *The Zone of Silence*, Avon Books, New York, 1987.

*Journal of Meteorology, U.K.**

*Journal of Science**

*Knowledge**

Mackal, Roy P., *Searching For Hidden Animals*, Doubleday & Co., Inc., New York, 1980.

*Meteorological Magazine**

*Monthly Weather Review**

*National Enquirer**

*Natural History**

*Natural Science**

*Nature**

*Notes and Queries**

Persinger, Michael A., Lafrenière, Gyslaine F., *Space-Time Transients and Unusual Events*, Nelson-Hall, Chicago, 1977.

Rogo, D. Scott, *Miracles: A Parascientific Inquiry Into Wondrous Phenomena*, The Dial Press, New York, 1982.

*Royal Meteorological Society Journal**

*Science**

*Science Digest**

*Scientific American**

*Smithsonian Institute Annual Reports**

*Symons's Monthly Meteorological Magazine**

*U.S. Geological Survey**

*Weather**

*Zoologist**